helmand

Helmand

- ▬▬▬ Roads
- ▬▬▬ District Border
- ▬▬▬ River
- ⊙ Provincial Center
- • City
- ⊢⊣ Dam

LOWER ELEVATION ▬▬▬▬▬ HIGHER ELEVATION

Ghor

Dai Kundi

Baghran

• Baghran

Uruzgan

Musa
Qala

Naw Zad

• Naw Zad

Musa
Qala •

Kajaki

Kajaki • ⊢⊣

Sangin

• Washer

• Sangin

Washer

Nahri
Sarraj

Gereshk •

Nad Ali •

Nad Ali

Lashkar
Gah •⊙

Lashkar
Gah

Lashkar
Gah •

Marja •

Nawa-i Barakzayi

Nawa-i Barakzayi

Nimroz

• Garmser

Kandahar

Garmser

Khanishin

• Khanishin

Dishu •

Dishu

Khanishin

Pakistan

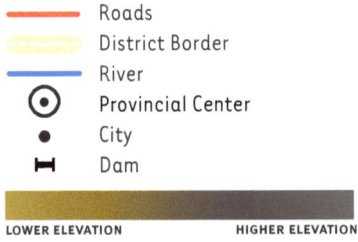

*Note: Although Marja has been made into a separate district from
Nad Ali, its exact boundaries had not been determined as of July 2010.*

Table of Contents

List of Tables and Maps

LIST OF TABLES

LIST OF MAPS

Acronyms and Key Terms

ABP	Afghan Border Police
ADT	Agribusiness Development Team
ANA	Afghan National Army
ANBP	Afghan National Border Police
ANDS	Afghan National Development Strategy
ANP	Afghan National Police
ANSF	Afghan National Security Forces
Arbakai	A volunteer, tribal police force which follows a strict ethical code
AWCC	Afghan Wireless Communication Company
BEFA	Basic Education for Afghanistan
BPHS	Basic Package of Health Services
CA	Civil Affairs
CDCs	Community Development Councils
CERP	Commander's Emergency Response Program
CHC	Comprehensive Health Center
COIN	Counterinsurgency
CSO	Central Statistics Office
DDS	District Development Shura
DIAG	Disbandment of Illegal Armed Groups
DoS	US Department of State
DST	District Support Team
FATA	Federally Administered Tribal Areas
GIRoA	Government of the Islamic Republic of Afghanistan
HIG or HIH	Hezb-e Islami Gulbuddin ("Islamic Party" formed by Gulbuddin Hekmatyar)

HIK	Hezb-e Islami Khalis ("Islamic Party" formed by Mohammad Yunus Khalis)
ICRC	International Committee of the Red Cross
IDLG	Independent Directorate for Local Governance
IED	Improvised Explosive Device
IO	International Organization
IRoA	Islamic Republic of Afghanistan
ISAF	International Security Assistance Force
ISI	Inter-Service Intelligence (Pakistan)
Karez	A small underground irrigation system popular in Afghanistan
LGCD	Local Governance and Community Development Program
Meshrano Jirga	Elders' Assembly, upper house of Afghan National Assembly
MRRD	Ministry of Rural Rehabilitation and Development
Mustafiat	Department of Finance
NDS	National Directorate for Security
NGO	Non-Governmental Organization
NSP	National Solidarity Program
NWFP	North West Frontier Province
Pashtunwali	The Pashtuns' pre-Islamic code of conduct
PC	Provincial Council
PDC	Provincial Development Council
PDP	Provincial Development Plan
PRT	Provincial Reconstruction Team
UN	United Nations
UNAMA	United Nations Assistance Mission in Afghanistan
UNOPS	United Nations Office for Project Services
USACE	US Army Corp of Engineers
USAID	US Agency for International Development
USDA	US Department of Agriculture
Wali	Governor
Wolesi Jirga	People's Assembly, lower house of Afghan National Assembly
Woluswal	District Administrator

Guide to the Handbook

This handbook is intended to be a concise field guide to Helmand for internationals deploying to the province. Using this guide will accelerate the orientation process and help you to better think about the challenges of Helmand province throughout your time in the field.

Key sources for this guide include official Islamic Republic of Afghanistan (IRoA), United Nations, and United States Government (USG) publications. This book also employs information and perspectives from Afghan and international experts who have spent significant time in Helmand.

The editors made every effort to ensure accuracy. It should be noted, however, that there is often considerable disagreement regarding what is "ground truth" in Helmand, and things are constantly changing. As such, consider this book part of your orientation, and not an all-inclusive source for everything you need to know. The best information will come from those individuals and organizations located in Helmand who know it inside and out. This handbook also suggests resources and organizations to further assist you. There is a list of recommended references and internet sites listed in the Appendix.

Information in this handbook is unclassified. The views and opinions expressed in this handbook are those of IDS International and in no way reflect the views of the United States Government or the United States Army.

HOW TO USE THE HANDBOOK

To help stabilize a community, it is necessary to understand its people, history, culture, economy, interests, and needs. Understanding the community will assist in the creation of a civil affairs strategy – in partnership with the Provincial Reconstruction Team (PRT) and the Afghans themselves – to address sources of instability in the province. Understanding the community and working effectively with local groups and governments can help isolate the insurgency from the population and lay the groundwork for lasting stability. It is essential not only to know who matters within a community, but also what type of assistance or engagement would be most effective, and what political compromises are possible.

Here are some questions that apply to engaging communities in this province:

- What are the influential groups in my area (tribal, political, business, etc.)?

- What are their interests and relationships? What do they care most about and why? What are their perceptions of themselves, their neighbors, the IRoA, and international forces/activities in their area?

- How can that community or group be more connected to the larger political process of creating a representative and responsive Afghan government? What political or economic issues must be addressed to create effective governance responsive to this community and to build community support for the political process?

- What are the sources of conflict or instability in this area? Are groups pursuing interests in a way that fosters conflict or undermines stability or governance? If so, why?

- Are you communicating with the right representatives of that group? How can you establish and maintain credibility with the group? How can you use your influence, operations, leverage, and resources to address sources of conflict and instability and to connect that community to the process of building a stable Afghanistan?

THE ELECTRONIC UPDATE

Look for electronic updates to this book at *www.idsinternational.net/afpakbooks*. Updates will cover new developments, issues, and leaders that emerge after publication. They will also provide corrections and expanded content in key areas based on input from readers.

We hope the handbook will continue to be a valuable tool in thinking about the challenges in Helmand. If you have questions, comments, or feedback for future updates or editions please email *afghanbooks@idsinternational.net*.

ABOUT IDS INTERNATIONAL

Publisher of Afghanistan Provincial Handbook Series

This book is part of a series of handbooks on Afghanistan provinces. Other titles include Nuristan, Laghman, Kunar, Nangahar, Kandahar, Paktika, Paktya, Khost, and Ghazni provinces. In addition to publishing these handbooks, IDS International provides training and analysis to government and private organizations in the areas of politics, economics, culture, stability operations, reconstruction, counterinsurgency, and interagency relations. In particular, IDS is a leading trainer of the US military in working with Provincial Reconstruction Teams (PRTs) in Iraq and

Afghanistan. IDS offers its clients expertise and experience in the difficult work of interagency collaboration in complex operations. The writers and editors on this project offer a lifetime of experience working in these provinces and share a dedication to bringing peace and prosperity to the people of Afghanistan.

Authors: Tom Westmacott, Pat Irish, and Nick Lockwood
Editors: Nick Dowling, Tom Praster, and Dana Stinson
Assistant Editors: Josh Adlakha, Emily Rose, and Tom Viehe

IDS INTERNATIONAL GOVERNMENT SERVICES
1916 Wilson Boulevard
Suite 302
Arlington, VA 22201
703-875-2212
www.idsinternational.net
afpakbooks@idsinternational.net

PUBLISHED: JULY 2010

This and other AfPak handbooks may be bought in either hard copy or digital format. Samples are available upon request. IDS International is also a leading provider of training and support on the cultural, political, economic, interagency and information aspects of conflict. For inquires, please email *afpakbooks@idsinternational.net* or call 703-875-2212.

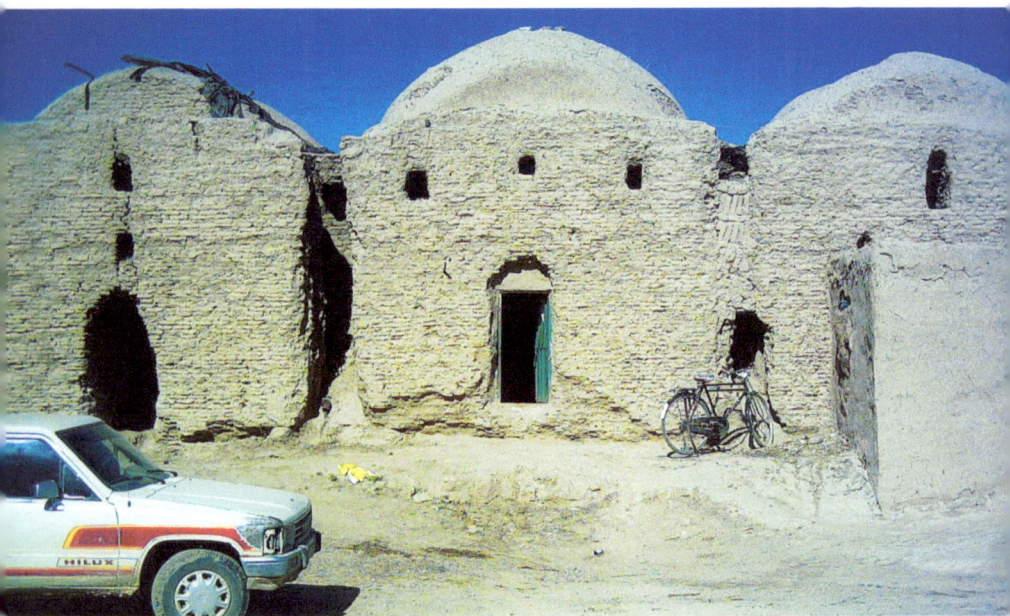

These 500 year old houses are still occupied today. This traditional style of houses in southern Helmand differs greatly from the modern houses built in Lashkar Gah in the 1950s through 1970s.

PHOTO BY PAT IRISH

Chapter 1
Overview and Orientation

The southern province of Helmand is a land of extremes. It is the largest province in Afghanistan, covering roughly 9 percent of the country – approximately half the size of RC East. Its main artery, the Helmand River, is the longest in Afghanistan, and potentially the most productive in terms of hydroelectric power and irrigation. In 2010, Helmand was the largest producer of narcotics in the world, surpassing all countries save its own.

Helmand stretches 445 kilometers north to south, making it the longest province in the country. It reaches temperatures of 120° F on its southern border in the summer and negative 20° F on its northern border in the winter. It has at one time experienced Afghanistan's closest association with modern Western culture and lifestyle (especially during the American development program of the 1950s-70s), but today it has become a stronghold for the insurgency against coalition reconstruction efforts in Afghanistan – led primarily by fighters representing the retrograde and repressive Taliban movement. Helmand is arguably the most volatile province in Afghanistan today.

Without the Helmand River, the province could not support its nearly 1.5 million people (this figure is based on a 2003 survey – some suggest the population is closer to a million). The river has made the desert productive; in the past, Helmand was the breadbasket of southern Afghanistan. Helmand's capital city, Lashkar Gah (known as "Lash" to expats and locals alike), is also a product of the river. The city was developed about fifty years ago by US and European engineers, aid workers, and their families who came to Afghanistan because of their enthusiasm for modernization and development.

The southern two-thirds of Helmand are sand-covered or stony desert, except for the fertile banks of the Helmand River and its canals. The northern third of the province rises precipitously from heights of 900 meters at the plains to heights of 3,000 meters at the northern border. Mountains separate Helmand from Ghor to the northwest and from Uruzgan to the northeast. Most of the population prior to the post-World War II development projects settled in what is today the northern tier of districts. Inhabited in large part by relatively conservative Durrani Pashtuns and Ghilzai Pashtuns, the province is beset by longstanding ethnic and tribal tensions. Some feuds have roots generations old that can reach down to the sub-tribal level. In addition, the wars, which have afflicted Afghanistan almost continuously since 1979, have left chronically ungoverned territories, isolated communities, and instability in the province.

The period of Russian rule in the 1980s saw some Helmandis join with the communists, while others supported the mujahedin resistance. In the 1990s, those same mujahedin groups fractured and fought a confused civil war which precipitated the rise of the Taliban and, ultimately, the arrival of Western forces in 2001.

Today, a relatively small percentage of Helmandis actively supports the Taliban; another minority actively supports the government and the coalition. Many are neutral, having adopted a survival strategy that has been learned and re-learned over 30 years of war. However, people need to sustain themselves, and as economic development slows, some pick up a gun for whoever will pay, becoming "economic insurgents." The Taliban have also adroitly manipulated historic tensions between the two Durrani tribal groups, the Zirak and the Panj-pai. Members of the disenfranchised Panj-pai tribes have been willingly co-opted into the Taliban as a means of addressing long-held grievances.

There is also an undercurrent of nostalgia for the Taliban days, particularly among ultra-conservative Pashtuns in rural areas, for whom security and freedom from crime and violence are top priorities. Growing disillusionment with the Kabul government's inefficiency, corruption, and predatory actions, together with the perceived failure of the international community to improve the lives of Afghans, reinforces this nostalgic tendency. Though life under the Taliban was harsh, austere, and without prospect of economic development, there was security and justice – albeit of a particularly brutal type.

Helmand has transformed since the end of 2007 and early 2008. The lowest point was the assassination of the deputy governor in Lashkar Gah. The security and governance situations are still challenging, but the arrival of significant numbers of additional international troops has created a more permissive environment for improved governance and social and economic development.

ORIENTATION

Helmand lies just west of Kandahar and east of Nimroz. To the north of Helmand sit the provinces of Farah, Ghor, Dai Kundi, and Uruzgan. The province has a 120-kilometer unprotected and unpatrolled border with Pakistan's Baluchistan province to the south. Helmand is 58,584 sq km and has a population between 1 and 1.5 million.

There is some commercial activity, but relatively little inter-tribal mixing with the northern neighbors, with the exception of Uruzgan. Ghor has a primarily Aimaq and Tajik population, and Dai Kundi is predominantly populated by ethnic Hazaras. Farah is thinly populated at the common border. Uruzgan and Kandahar, on the other hand, are closely related by ethnic, tribal, family, economic, and commercial interests. There is little contact with Nimroz to the west, whose population is clustered on the opposite side of the province, and whose population is a mix of Pashto and Dari speakers influenced by a proximity to Iran.

The rugged terrain of the north encourages local autonomy and allows for the movement of insurgents. The uncontrolled border on the south sees rampant smuggling of commercial goods, weapons, and drugs. It has also facilitated the free passage of weapons and fighters for anti-government elements.

Districts

There are now 14 districts in Helmand province, including the capital district of Lashkar Gah (See Table 1). Following Operation Moshtarak in February 2010, Marja was established as a district separate from Nad Ali. Although no decision has been taken by Kabul to legally establish Marja district's borders, these will likely be in place by the September 2010 parliamentary elections. In addition, some district boundaries are new in the last few years, and others are not clearly defined. The situation has dramatically improved since the low point at the end of 2007. District governors under the direct control of the provincial government now exist in 10 districts, supported by District Stabilization Teams (DSTs), ISAF forces, and an embryonic presence from line ministries.

The terrain of the northern tier of districts runs from the hard-scrabble, barren plains and abrupt outbreak of rugged mountains in Washer in the west, through the increasingly habitable mountain valleys of Naw Zad, Musa Qala, Kajaki, and on to the splendid isolation of Baghran district in the northeast.

The central tier of districts includes Nahre Sarraj (Gereshk), Sangin, Nad Ali, Lashkar Gah, and Nawa y Barakzayi. These districts were the main beneficiaries of the irrigation schemes of 30-50 years ago. Population increases, particularly in Nad Ali and Lashkar Gah, resulted from the resettlement of landless peasants and Kuchi nomads from other provinces. Many of these were from the east, resulting in the mixture of Ghilzai Pashtun tribes and non-tribal Pashtuns found in the area today. A further wave arrived in the 1990s, including many Pashtun refugees, displaced from inter-ethnic fighting in Faryab and other northern provinces during the civil war or Taliban periods.

The southern tier includes Garmser, Reg, and Dishu. The north part of Garmser resembles the central area in population mix and density, but only where there is engineered irrigation. Southern Garmser and most of Dishu are populated by the Baluch, a non-Pashtun ethnic group with commercial and kinship ties to Baluchistan, who are more oriented to the other side of the porous Pakistani border than to Helmand or Afghanistan. Pashtuns occupy a narrow band along the Helmand as it turns west to cross Nimroz province and expires in the Sistan marshes on the border with Iran.

Key Towns

Lashkar Gah and Gereshk are the most developed towns in the province. They are municipalities which have a certain degree of autonomy. Sangin is probably the next most populated "urban" area. It has a history of close association with the narcotics trade, and most recently as the largest town held by the Taliban.

The provincial capital, **Lashkar Gah** (estimated population 250,000), is an attractive city on the banks of the Helmand River about 60 km south of the Ring Road (Highway 1). Lashkar Gah means "home of the soldiers," and it was originally the garrison for the soldiers and elephant army of the 11th century Ghaznavid Dynasty. It is the seat of international and Afghan government presence in the province.

Its distinct appearance resulted from the fact that it was designed and built by Americans in the 1950s-1970s and involved the construction and maintenance of the Kajaki Dam and the creation of the Helmand Valley Authority (later the Helmand-Arghandab Valley Authority, or HAVA). The brickwork of suburban America contrasts with the mud-walled homes typical of the region and the green glass and reinforced concrete "narco-tecture" of palaces built recently by local smugglers.

Also found here are the governor's compound, the court house, the state bank, a park and a stadium, other government buildings, the state-owned Bost Hotel (Russian Officers Quarters, 1980-1989), a gorgeous alabaster mosque, and the huge HAVA building and complex. Although there is a more traditional side to the city, much of the city is laid out in a grid with wide streets, many of them asphalt which is unusual in Afghanistan.

Lashkar Gah was relatively secure as of April 2010, although security has deteriorated significantly in recent months in the districts due west of the city and in outlying areas.

Gereshk (estimated population 180,000), the former capital of Helmand, is strategically located on Highway 1 at the junction with the Helmand River. Given its location, the city is a traditional center of trade, serving as a gateway to the north of the province. To the north of Gereshk, the river valley leads to Sangin.

Sangin (estimated population 50,000) has the reputation of being a wide open city with a sprawling bazaar and has recently become renowned for its drug market. It has a history of tribal, political, and drug-related violence. In 2006 through 2009, Sangin gained attention as the site of back-and-forth battles between British ISAF forces and the Taliban, resulting in significant damage to the town. ISAF has secured the town, but has not gained control of the surrounding countryside. The river valley from Gereshk to Sangin was the scene of regular fighting during 2006 and 2007. In late 2007 and early 2008, UK, Danish, and Afghan forces constructed a large number of small bases in this cultivated "Green Zone."

Garmser (estimated population 15,000). Much like Sangin, the Garmser District Center has become familiar in the news as a result of the battles of both British forces and US Marines to take, retake, and attempt to hold it from the Taliban. The security bubble is advancing south of the district center and new elections for the District Community Council will soon follow.

Marja (estimated population 60,000). The Marja area of Nad Ali was liberated from Taliban control by the US Marine Corps in February 2010. Clearing operations began on 13 February, the Afghan flag was raised over the District Center on 25 February, and on 7 March President Karzai made Marja a separate district.

Musa Qala (estimated population 20,000). The major settlement in the north of the province, Musa Qala has a large bazaar which was devastated during protracted fighting with UK forces in 2006. For 10 months in 2007, the town was held by the Taliban, which had violated a non-aggression pact with local leaders, but ISAF and Afghan forces retook it in December 2007. UK forces installed a former Taliban commander as the local governor and hold the town and several kilometers around it. It now falls within the US area of responsibility.

Map 1.
Population Map of Helmand

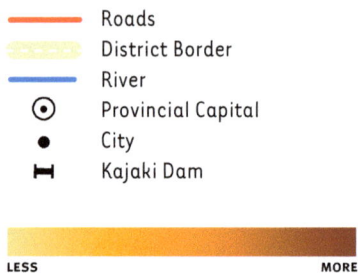

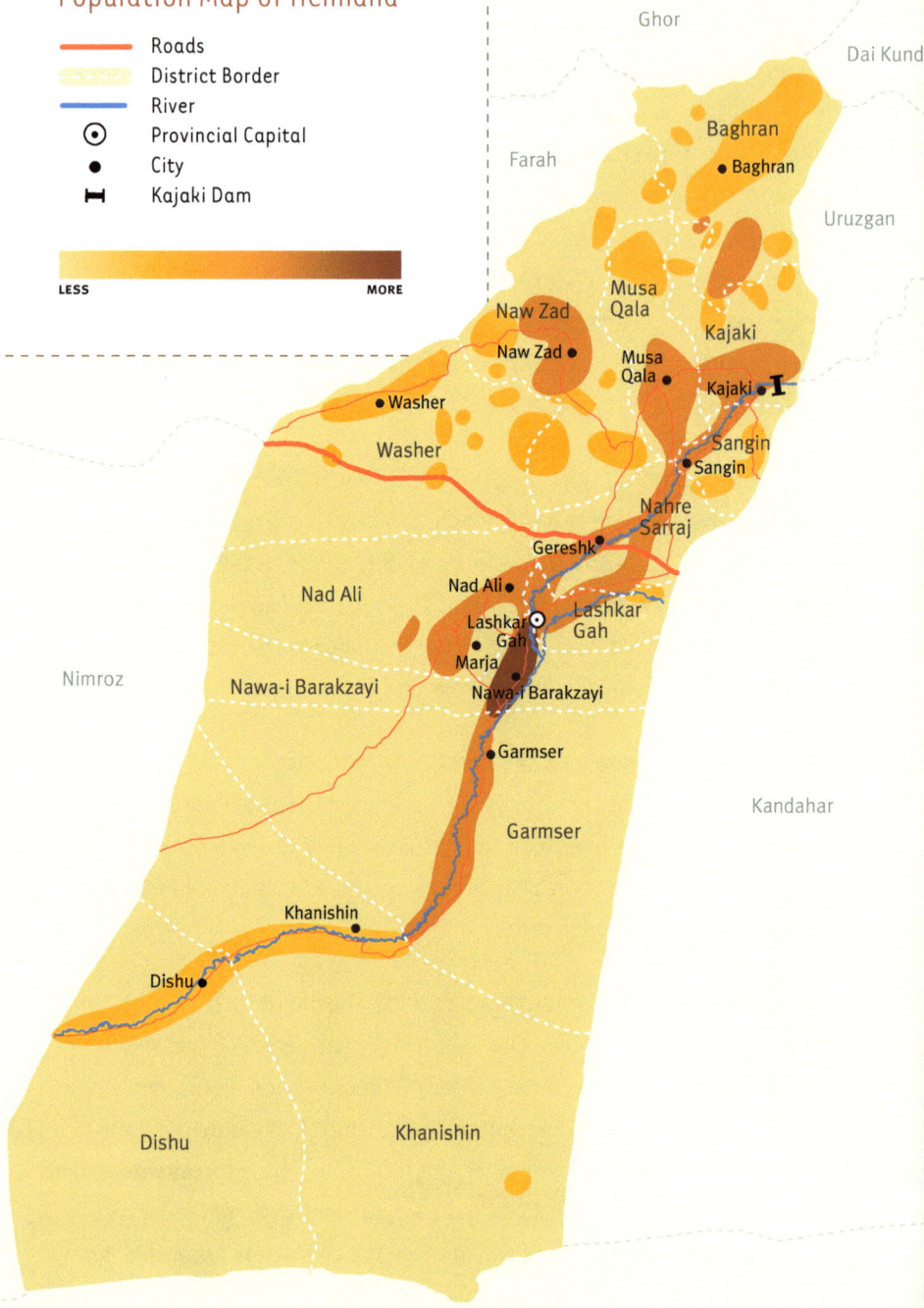

- —— Roads
- ——— District Border
- —— River
- ⊙ Provincial Capital
- ● City
- I Kajaki Dam

LESS ▭ MORE

Ghor

Dai Kund

Farah

Baghran
● Baghran

Uruzgan

Musa
Qala

Kajaki

Naw Zad
● Naw Zad

Musa
Qala ●

Kajaki ●

● Washer

Sangin
● Sangin

Washer

Nahre
Sarraj

Gereshk ●

Nad Ali ●

Nad Ali

Lashkar
Gah ⊙

Lashkar
Gah

Nimroz

Marja ●

Nawa-i Barakzayi

Nawa-i Barakzayi

Kandahar

● Garmser

Garmser

Khanishin ●

● Dishu

Dishu

Khanishin

Pakistan

Table 1: District Populations

DISTRICT	CENTER	POPULATION	MAJOR TRIBES
Baghran	Baghran	100,000	Alizai
Washer	Washer	30,000	Noorzai
Naw Zad	Naw Zad	100,000	Alizai, Barakzai, Noorzai
Musa Qala	Musa Qala	120,000	Alizai
Kajaki	Kajaki	100,000	Alizai
Nahre Sarraj	Gereshk	200,000	Isakzai, Barakzai
Sangin	Sangin	65,000	Isakzai,
Nad Ali	Nad Ali	175,000	Ghilzai, Non-tribal, Minorities
Marja	Marja	Approx 60,000	Noorzai, minorities
Lashkar Gah	Lashkar Gah	250,000	Popolzai, Barakzai, Minorities
Nawa-i Barakzayi	Nawa-i Barakzayi	90,000	Popolzai, Noorzai
Garmser	Hazarjoft	100,000	Noorzai, Ghilzai, Achakzai, Baluch
Khanishin	Khanishin	20,000	Barech, Baluch
Dishu	Dishu	20,000	Baluch
Total		**1,430,000**	

Note: There are approximately 60 main Pashtun tribes and 400 sub-tribes. See Chapter 2.

All of the district centers are important seats of government, and are usually the apex for any available public services, including areas of health, education, and commerce. District centers, having been in constant contention with insurgents, have also served as symbols of victory and defeat for both coalition and insurgent forces over the last few years.

RELEVANT HISTORICAL ISSUES

Pre-Modern History (Pre-1979)

Archeologists have identified agricultural communities from as early as the fourth millennium BC in Helmand. Since that time, Helmand has been host to a number of invaders, including Alexander the Great, the Ghaznavid Dynasty, the Ghorid Dynasty, Ghengis Khan, and Timur.

The British made inroads into Helmand on several occasions in the 19th century while playing the "Great Game" with Russia. Most significantly, in July 1880, the army of Ayub Khan of Herat defeated a British force in the Battle of Maiwand near the Helmand-Kandahar border in which nearly 1,000 British soldiers perished. The perceived defeat of Britain in three separate imperialist wars has bolstered the fiercely independent character of Afghans. These invasions have created a particular mistrust of Great Britain in the province today.

After the Second World War, the US and Europe financed a number of development programs in Helmand. The Communist takeover in the 1970s, however, resulted in the exodus of Western developmental aid, and led to the Soviet invasion and occupation in 1979. Older Helmandis continue to have respect for the US role in developing the province pre-1979 and remember that era as one of peace and prosperity.

Communist Era (1979-1992)

The Communist hold on Helmand did not extend far outside of Lashkar Gah, as various *jihadi* insurgent groups made life in the hinterland unpleasant. This period witnessed the breakdown of already limited state institutions and the devastation of the rural economy as food production drastically fell. There was little to no funding for education, health, and other government services.

The Communists significantly eroded the traditional power structures of Helmand by driving the khans – landed notables who served as intermediaries between the people and the government – off their land. *Jihadi* figures, in turn, filled the power vacuum. One such leader, Nasim Akhundzada, brought poppy cultivation – which had previously been restricted to the north – to Helmand in order to fund and support his troops.

Two other major militia leaders also emerged from Helmand: Abdul Wahid (also known as Rais Baghrani) in Baghran and Abdul Rahman Jan. The three insurgent groups fought the Communist government, the Soviets, and each other while courting support from major mujahedin parties that received US funding to fight the Soviets. After the Soviet withdrawal, Nasim Akhundzada continued to spread his poppy empire throughout the province. In 1990, he was killed while visiting Pakistan in a hit presumably ordered by Hekmatyar. His brothers, Rasul and Ghaffar, took over his position.

Mujahedin and Taliban (1992-2001)

After the Communist government fell in 1993, Rasul Akhundzada pushed the remaining communists out of Lashkar Gah and proclaimed himself governor. The Taliban arrived in Helmand in 1994 and forced Rasul and his son, Sher Mohammad Akhundzada, into exile in

Peshawar. Rais Baghrani stayed in his Baghran redoubt and eventually became a Taliban commander.

Contemporary Events (2001-Present)

When the Taliban retreated from Helmand, Abdul Rahman Jan (ARJ) and his Noorzai militia liberated Lashkar Gah, and Sher Mohammad Akhundzada became governor with the support of President Karzai. Dad Mohammad Khan (DMK) emerged from Sangin to become chief of the Helmand National Department of Security (NDS). Mir Wali in Gereshk remained commander of his militia, which gained recognition from the Ministry of Defense. Rais Baghrani , who had reportedly sheltered Mullah Omar after his flight from Kandahar, hid from US forces in Baghran. The odd foursome of rivals – Sher Mohammad (Alizai), ARJ (Noorzai), DMK (Alokazai) and Mir Wali (Barakzai) kept Helmand from any serious outbreaks of violence for four years and aggressively opposed the Taliban. DMK had a reputation for treating Taliban in his custody with extreme cruelty. Certainly, however, the relative stability that Helmand experienced during those years implied some arrangements had been made with the Taliban at a local level.

By 2005, the political balance began unraveling. Mir Wali's troops were disarmed under the Disarmament, Demobilization, Reintegration (DDR) Program, DMK and ARJ were removed from their posts, and Sher Mohammad was removed as governor at the behest of the British.

Taliban infiltration of the province appears to have resumed as early as 2002. Many Helmandis claim that Governor Sher Mohammed accelerated the process by fanning tribal tensions and dabbling in the drug trade. From March 2005, violent incidents began to increase steadily. By the time the British Battle Group under ISAF Command arrived, it faced open warfare.

In recent years, British and Afghan forces deployed farther out into the districts in attempts to extend security, leading to a series of battles with Taliban forces around Musa Qala, Sangin, and Garmser. Further increases in ISAF and Afghan forces were not able to significantly roll back Taliban control. British forces built a large number of small forward operating bases in the "Green Zone" between Gereshk and Sangin in an attempt to counter continued Taliban influence. In May 2008, the 24th MEU was deployed to Garmser. It overran Taliban positions and established a new frontline approximately 7 km south of the district center.

Through 2009 and early 2010, further US Marine forces surged into Helmand. A Marine Expeditionary Brigade arrived in 2009 and was enhanced to a Marine Expeditionary Force (MEF). The key operation of 2010 was Operation Moshtarak in February, when US Marine units, supported by the elements of an Army Stryker Brigade and the British Task Force, successfully cleared the populous Marja area of Nad Ali. 1 MEF are now established in Helmand and will take operational control of the British Task Force Helmand in June 2010. The MEF will then stand up as the new regional command, RC South-West, with initial responsibility for Helmand and Nimroz provinces.

Elders from northern Marja meet during a shura held at Combat Outpost Coutu. Working with the local tribes and respecting customs and traditional methods is essential to effective political and development work in Helmand.

PHOTO BY CPL. MEGAN SINDELAR

Chapter 2
Ethnicity, Tribes,
Language, and Religion

ETHNICITY

Pashtuns constitute the overwhelming majority in Helmand. The Baluch
are found almost exclusively in the southernmost part of the province,
bordering the Baluchistan province of Pakistan. Other ethnic groups,
each constituting less than one percent of the population, are Tajik,
Hazara, and a small Indian population of Sikhs, all concentrated in
Lashkar Gah and, to a lesser extent, in Nad Ali and Garmser. The center
and south have attracted non-Pashtun outsiders such as Hazaras,
Tajiks, and Uzbeks from the north of the country as the new irrigation
systems made more land available for occupation and cultivation.

Kuchis are not an ethnic group, but are identified primarily by their
lifestyle – they are nomads who lead a seasonal, migratory existence
following their herds of sheep or goats. Most of the Helmand kuchis are
Baluch in the south and Pashtun in the north.

Table 2. Major Pashtun Tribes in Helmand

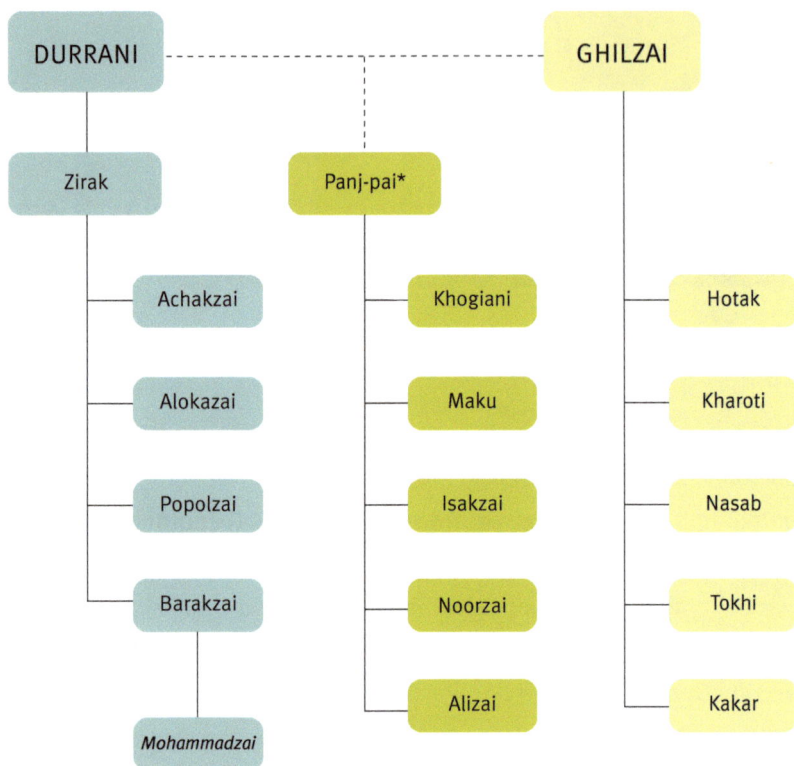

DURRANI		GHILZAI
Zirak	**Panj-pai***	
Achakzai	Khogiani	Hotak
Alokazai	Maku	Kharoti
Popolzai	Isakzai	Nasab
Barakzai	Noorzai	Tokhi
Mohammadzai	Alizai	Kakar

* Some tribal charts show the Durrani confederacy encompassing the Zirak and Panj-pai groups of tribes, but others categorize the Panj-pai as members of the Ghilzai confederacy. Experience in southern Afghanistan suggests Panj-pai sometimes describe themselves as Ghilzais if they oppose the government, or call themselves Durranis if they accept the government.

TRIBES

An anthropological textbook would describe the tribe as the most powerful facet of Pashtun society. It provides an informal governmental framework. Tribal society works on a group decision-making structure rather than an individual decision-making structure. All decisions for the tribe or sub-sections within a tribe would be determined as a group by the tribal elders, who tend to be local khans (large landowners) and *maliks* (influential community leaders with quasi-official status). The goal of justice would be to promote group harmony rather than punish an individual.

There are two primary mechanisms for tribal elders to make decisions. The first is called a *jirga*, which is a meeting held to make a specific decision. It can involve people from within or outside of the tribe. Any decision made in a jirga is binding.

The other meeting type is called a *shura*, from the Arabic word for consultation. Shuras seek to redress wrongs through arbitration, and address issues of pride and reparations more than they actually impose punishment. After decades of war, shuras have become more militarized in Afghanistan, acting as short-term advisory councils that can include elders, commanders, and landowners.

With Afghanistan's history of difficulty in establishing a stable central government that reaches down to the local level, the traditional tribal structures remain the principal organizer of the society.

However, these tribal structures do not function so neatly in Helmand. The 1950s settlement of the then newly irrigated central belt led to a mix of Pashtun tribes living side by side. Traditional tribal mechanisms further broke down under the Communist rule and Soviet occupation. Thirty years of war saw the emergence of a number of

Map 2. Tribal Map of Helmand

Legend:
- Alizai
- Barakzai
- Barech
- Baluch
- Noorzai
- Alokazai
- Isakzai
- None
- Mixed Ghilzai
- Non-tribal
- Popolzai
- Minority of Turkmen, Tajiks, Hazaras & Hindus

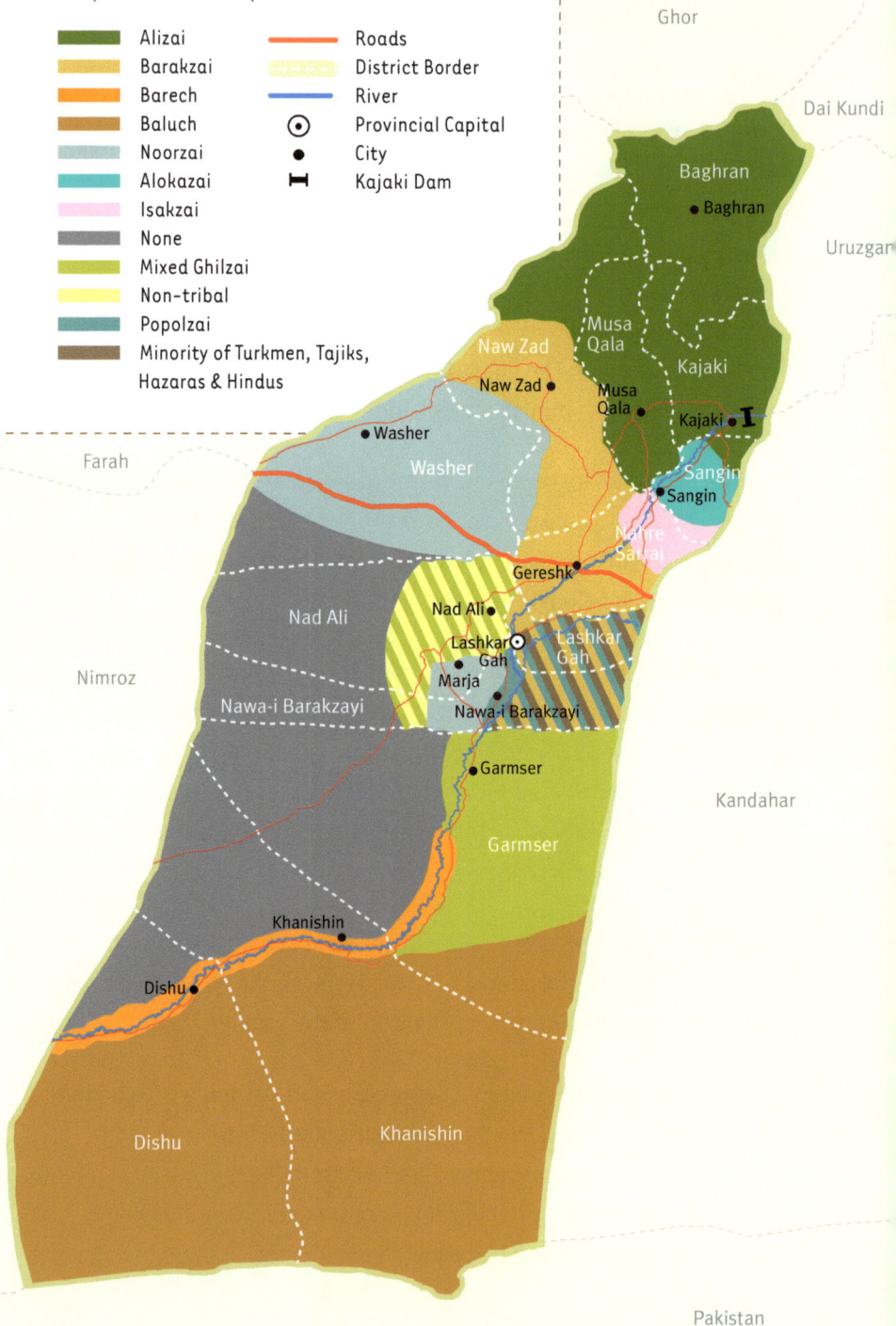

- Roads
- District Border
- River
- ⊙ Provincial Capital
- • City
- Ⅰ Kajaki Dam

Ghor

Dai Kundi

Uruzgan

Baghran
• Baghran

Musa Qala

Kajaki

Naw Zad
Naw Zad •

Musa Qala •

Kajaki •
Ⅰ

• Washer

Washer

Sangin
• Sangin

Nahre Saraj

Gereshk •

Farah

Nad Ali
Nad Ali •

Lashkar Gah ⊙
• Gah
Marja •

Lashkar Gah

Nawa-i Barakzayi

Nawa-i Barakzayi

Nimroz

• Garmser

Garmser

Garmser

Kandahar

Khanishin •

Dishu •

Dishu

Khanishin

Pakistan

"tribal strongmen" of which Sher Mohammed Akhunzada of the Alizai sub-tribe, the Hasanzai, is an example. While they are limited to dominance over one tribal group, they still have subverted the traditional Pashtun deliberation processes. This was further accentuated by the Taliban's active promotion of the mullah as the sole source of authority, rather than a balance of influence between the mullahs, khans, and maliks.

Ten Pashtun tribes make up 94 percent of the population of Helmand, with the tribes divided into two confederations or super-tribes – the Durrani and Ghilzai. The vast majority of Pashtun are Durrani, with a smaller number identified as Ghilzai. The tribes with a longer history in the province tend to be found in the north.

The Durrani are the most politically dominant federation and have ruled Afghanistan continuously since 1747 with two exceptions: during the Communist era and the Taliban era, the Ghilzai Pashtuns had greater political influence.

The largest grouping of tribes within the Durrani confederation is the **Zirak**. The Zirak consists of three smaller tribes which dominate the government. They are the **Popolzai** (the tribe of Hamid Karzai), the **Barakzai**, and the **Alokazai**.

The **Mohammadzai**, a sub-tribe of the Barakzai, produced all the leaders of Afghanistan between 1747 and 1978 (barring one nine month period in 1929). Another tribe, the **Achakzai**, is also included in the Zirak; it was originally a sub-tribe of the Barakzai, but was given the separate status of a tribe by the first Afghan king Ahmad Shah Durrani in an attempt to weaken the Barakzai tribe. Since 2001, the Zirak tribes have again gained a dominant position within the government in the south.

The **Panj-pai**, or "Five Fingers," are alternately classified as members of the Ghilzai or Durrani confederacies. It is made up of the **Noorzai, Isakzai, Khogiani, Alizai,** and **Maku** sub-tribes, which are smaller and less influential than the larger Zirak tribes.

Members of the Panj-pai sometimes describe themselves as Ghilzai if they oppose the government, or as Durrani if they accept the government. On the whole, there is considerable evidence that the Panj-pai are better represented in the insurgency than the Zirak.

The Ghilzai live primarily along the eastern border region, and there are four Ghilzai tribes with strong representation in the southwest of Afghanistan: the **Hotak, Nasab, Tokhi,** and **Kharoti**. The Hotak is the tribe of Taliban leader Mullah Omar. Mullah Dadullah Akhund, the most prominent Taliban commander in Helmand in 2006 until his death in 2007, and Mullah Mansoor Dadullah, his brother and successor, were both from a small Ghilzai sub-tribe, the **Kakar**.

Qawm

Southern Afghan culture is primarily a system of interlocking and overlapping networks, based on ties of kinship, religion, tribe, ethnicity, locality, patronage, and common interests. These networks revolve around powerful individuals who bind followers to them through patronage, thereby elevating their status and establishing bonds of reciprocal obligation among their followers. Such a network is referred to as a *qawm*, and it is the chief building block of Afghan society. An Afghan's qawm includes his family, clan, tribe, and network of associates. An Afghan can invoke his qawm in support of what might be a purely individual dispute, thereby calling a small army to his side. The ideas that underpin the notion of qawm are rooted in the Pashtun honor code of *pashtunwali*. A Pashtun can go to war for many reasons, but at the root of most Afghan conflicts are the objects upon which a man's honor rests: "Zan, Zar, Zemin," "Women, Gold, Land."

Pashtunwali

Society in Helmand is very conservative, strictly religious, and structured around "pashtunwali," which is the code of ethics for the Pashtun tribe. Pashtunwali means "the way of the Pashtuns," and is a pre-Islamic code of conduct followed by the Pashtun tribes. All Pashtuns have some knowledge of the code, and will try to follow it. Some tribes are stricter about the code than others. The four main parts of pashtunwali are as follows:

Nang (Honor): All parts of pashtunwali lead to honor. All Pashtuns are required to uphold the honor of their family and their tribe by following the other parts of the code. An insult to someone's tribe or family can lead to *badal* (see below). The biggest disputes are over women, land, and money, and a Pashtun man must protect these three things with his life and honor.

Melmastia (Hospitality): Pashtuns are known for their hospitality, and will go to great lengths to treat their guest with honor and respect. Most villages and large families will have a dedicated guesthouse. Even if a family has limited resources, a stranger will still be welcomed, fed and given a place to sleep. This applies to non-Pashtuns as well.

Nanawatay (Sanctuary): If one Pashtun has insulted another, or committed some crime, they are allowed to admit their guilt and ask for forgiveness. They will take gifts to the offended party and ask that the past be forgotten. The insulted party is then obligated to accept their offer. Often the women of a family or tribe will arrange for this to happen because women are seen as natural peacemakers. Nanawatay can also be used to beg for mercy and protection.

Badal (Revenge): Pashtuns are quick to take revenge for an insult, or seek justice for a past crime. It does not matter if the insult is decades old. The only way to restore honor to the family/clan/tribe is to exact revenge on the other family/clan/tribe.

THE TALIBAN AND TRIBAL STRUCTURE

The Taliban was established as a Pashtun Islamic movement which had no interest in tribal alliances. The early Talibs were defined primarily by their shared backgrounds as students of *madrassas* (religious schools) and their networks were established across tribal boundaries. (The word Talib literally means "religious student.")

Pashtuns who felt themselves excluded from power, particularly those in the Ghilzai tribes, were attracted to the Taliban's ideals and were better represented than the Durranis in the Taliban government from 1996 to 2001. Also, small tribes such as the Isakzai and the Kakar appeared to be better represented within the Helmand Taliban. However, not all members of these tribes were Taliban supporters.

The significance of tribal identity appears to have increased during the war years as people came to see it as a form of shared identity and security amid great uncertainty. At the same time, the figures who acted as the mediators between the tribes and the center, the khans and the tribal elders, have been increasingly sidelined.

In their place, if one looks at a list of the prominent figures in Helmand since 2001, one finds most of the powerbrokers are former jihadist commanders (known to some as warlords) who rose to prominence in the 1980s and 1990s.

LANGUAGES

The preferred language of 94 percent of Helmand's inhabitants is Pashto. While there are a few communities where Dari or Balochi is the first language, Pashto is the common language across Helmand. It is not uncommon to encounter bi- and tri-lingual Afghans in Helmand, especially among the educated. Urdu and/or Dari are quite common second languages, and a few individuals have some capability in all three, plus English. Older Helmandis, who grew up during the time of American development in the province, often have some knowledge of English.

Literacy: Helmand has one of the lowest literacy rates in Afghanistan. The literacy rate among males over the age of 25 is 20 percent and among women it is 11 percent; nationally it is 32 percent and 13 percent, respectively.

ROLE OF RELIGION

Islam is culturally important to most Afghans in Helmand, and the invocation of God pervades almost every conversation. Even if a person is not truly pious, he will at least appear to be. No outsider should ever speak poorly about Islam or accuse an Afghan of being un-Islamic. It is good to compliment someone for being a good Muslim, but the topic of religion should be approached lightly, if at all. Since the Koran is seen by Muslims as an infallible document, delivered to the Prophet directly by God, any debate on particulars of Islamic belief and practice should not be entered into.

Mullahs have a special place of influence over the people. Since Afghanistan is an Islamic Republic, there is no separation between religion and government. A law must be in line with Islamic principles for it to be accepted. The Director of Religious Affairs (officially called

Helmandi children dressed in traditional clothing celebrate the opening of the Lashkar Gah Provincial Reconstruction Team (PRT). Working with the local tribes and respecting customs and traditions is essential to effective political and development work in Helmand.

PHOTO BY PAT IRISH

Director of Haj and Awkaf) is the government's official representative, while the chairman of the ulema council will represent the mullahs in the province. Technically, these officials have some influence over the mullahs throughout the districts and are considered the "mouthpiece" of the mullah community. However, in Helmand, their reach is limited by the instability associated with the insurgency and the poor transport infrastructure.

The language of Islam is not the vernacular in Afghanistan, unlike the Arabian peninsula. Of the estimated 23,000 mullahs in Helmand, only 13,000 have received some form of religious education beyond rote learning the Koran in Arabic. The Taliban have established themselves as a source of authority and interpretation, and many mullahs will not challenge the Taliban's view because they are either intimidated or incapable of doing so. In rural areas, mullahs are a reflection of their environment, lacking education and sophistication. Mullahs can be a force multiplier for misinformation; rumor, no matter how improbable, finds no ground more fertile than in southern Afghanistan. Since mullahs are so influential, it is important to reach out to them either directly or through their hierarchy.

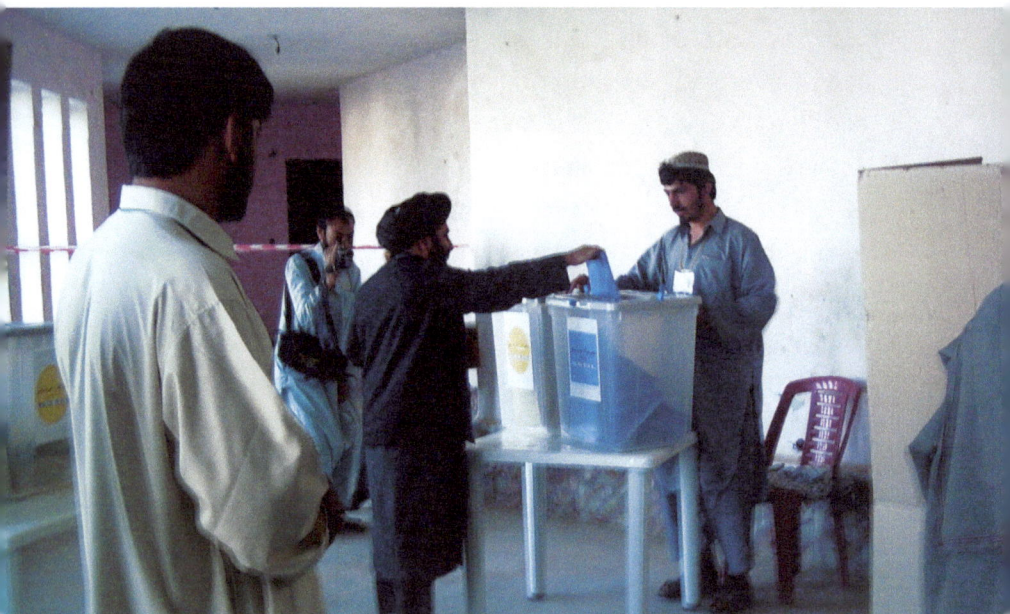

Former Governor of Helmand Sher Mohammed Akhundzada casts his vote on election day in September 2005. His family has dominated Helmand politics since the 1980s through tribal politicking, ruthless suppression of opponents and astute exploitation of the drugs trade. He served as governor from 2001 to December 2005.

PHOTO BY SPC. DANIEL LOVE

Chapter 3
Government and Leadership

After a period of disjointed and often weak leadership, Governor Mangal has brought stable governance to Helmand. Sher Mohammad Akhundzada was one of the longest serving governors, from December 2001 to December 2005, but he was replaced at the insistence of the British. Two successors, Mohammad Daud and Asadullah Wafa, both governed for approximately one year. Anxious for stability, Karzai appointed Gulab Mangal, who had been an effective governor of Laghman and Paktika in March 2008. Independent of family or tribal ties in Helmand, Mangal was tasked with reducing corruption in the province. District governance has expanded as security has improved, at least in the central belt from Garmser district center up to Gereshk.

HOW THE GOVERNMENT OFFICIALLY WORKS

Central Control

Authority and power in Afghanistan are concentrated in the national government as a means to counter the power of warlords in the provinces. As such, the provincial government is limited to an advisory role for the central government, while decisions on everything from policy to funding priorities are made in Kabul.

Provincial Government

A governor (*wali*) heads the provincial government and reports to the president through the Independent Directorate for Local Government (IDLG). A deputy and several staff that oversee provincial government management assist him.

Ministries in Kabul execute their policies and programs through departments located at the provincial level. Ministers, with the approval of the president, appoint provincial directors who manage the department. The director reports to and receives funds from the ministry in Kabul. The governor does not have budgetary authority over any of these departments, but must approve all expenditures before they are processed by the Department of Finance (*Mustafiat*).

The Provincial Council (PC), elected at the provincial level, provides a voice for the people in advising on provincial issues. The PC reports directly to the president and has no budget. Its relevance is largely dependent on the governor's support and on its members' individual resources and initiatives.

The Provincial Development Committee (PDC), including the governor and department heads, is responsible for creating the Provincial Development Plan (PDP) and coordinating with key players on development needs. External players such as the UN, PRT, and NGOs also attend meetings.

District and Local Governance

Government at the district level mirrors the provincial government with the *woluswal* (district governor), police chief, National Directorate of Security officer, clerks and a small police force. Ministry sub-departments also operate at the district level, but are not present in every district.

In Helmand, the Afghan Social Outreach Program has formed District Community Councils (DCCs) in Nad Ali, Nawa, Gereshk, and Gamsir, with more to follow in 2010. Five members of the Gereshk Community Council are female. These are transitional representative bodies, formed under the Sub-National Governance Policy, but not the constitution. An election shura, composed of appointed individuals, elects up to 45 of its number to form the DCC. The DCC has responsibility for drafting and then sustaining the District Development Plan (DDP), which identifies the priorities for reconstruction and development. They also have Prisoner Release, Security, and Justice sub-committees. They will transition to fully elected assemblies, but this is not expected to occur for a number of years. The National Solidarity Program (NSP), which forms Community Development Councils (CDCs), has not been a success in Helmand – due to a weak implementing partner and a hostile security environment.

The municipalities of Lashkar Gah and Gereshk are led by a mayor appointed by the president in consultation with the governor. Municipalities are independent from the provincial government, are free to plan, fund and implement projects, and can tax local businesses.

HOW IT ACTUALLY WORKS

Official governance is still challenging in Helmand, but it has improved in the last two years. Appointed district governors with staffs and a variety of ministerial representatives exist in 10 districts. The limits of their authority vary, but there were only five in 2006. In the central belt of Nawa, Nad Ali, Lashkar Gah, and Gereshk, the rule of the government covers most of the populated areas: in Sangin, Marja, and Garmser it is challenged; in Musa Qala, Now Zad, and Khanishin, it extends as far as the district center. There are no official district governors in Baghran, Washir, Kajaki, and Dishu. Outside the government's footprint, Helmand is governed by tribal authority as well as the influence of powerful tribal strongmen like Abdul Rahman Jan in Marja and Dad Mohammad Khan in Sangin. For more on tribal rule and customs, see Chapter 2.

Political power across Helmand is a competition between Governor Mangal, the Taliban, and the traditional anti-Taliban tribal strongmen of Helmand – most notably Sher Mohammad Akhundzada and Abdul Rahman Jan. Akhundzada, the former governor, strives to replace Mangal as governor despite his ties to narcotics and tribal violence. Akhundzada and his allies note that the Taliban have gained strength in Helmand since his departure. Shifting alliances and cutting political deals have always been essential elements of Helmand political life and remain so today as Taliban and anti-Taliban leaders vie for power.

The line ministries of the central government in Helmand have almost no function in the execution of services. Currently, there are 26 line ministries which vary in quality. Some are staffed by individuals with little or no technocratic expertise. Historically, the ministries were used by successive governors to balance competing tribal and political interest groups; as such, they represent a series of fiefdoms to provide what jobs and limited resources are available to their constituents.

A few of the line ministries are regarded as functional on some basic level by British officials in Helmand. The Ministry of Rural Rehabilitation and Development (MRRD) is the best and received $52 million in direct funding from 2006-08 from the British government.

The Health Ministry is also operating, with the assistance of international organizations, with some degree of competence and legitimacy. It is seen as less corrupt than the other ministries, chiefly because its doctors are able to supplement their income by running private health clinics outside office hours. This reduces their dependence on corruption to supplement poor government wages.

The Provincial Council has limited influence and members credit Governor Mangal with far greater engagement with the provincial council than his predecessors. The Provincial Development Committee process has not been effective, but the District Community Councils have assumed their roles where they exist.

SECURITY FORCES

Afghan National Army (ANA)

The ANA is perhaps the most functional and developed Afghan institution. As of April 2010, the ANA was close to 107,000 strong and training more at a rate of one kandak (battalion) per week. Following the 2010 London Conference, it is currently set to reach a goal of approximately 171,000 by the end of 2011. The Afghan ministry of defense tries to reflect the ethnic balance of the country within its armed forces, but Tajiks and Pashtuns are over-represented in the officer class and Hazaras and other minorities are significantly under-represented. Though Pashtuns are well represented in the army, they tend to come from the eastern provinces (the traditional recruitment area of the army) and not from the south. The key deficiency suffered by the ANA is a chronic lack of educated leaders and bureaucrats. With very low literacy levels, the ANA struggles to find officers who can read and bureaucrats to arrange logistics. Planning at every level is weak.

The ANA has participated in a number of important counterinsurgency operations in Helmand, including the retaking of Musa Qala in December 2007, Garmser in the summer of 2008, and the 2010 liberation of Marja. Its performance in these operations was professional, and its presence helped create an atmosphere of security following the operations. The ANA is the key partner, together with the Afghan Uniformed Police, in delivering the security necessary to allow civil development. A relative success in Helmand, the ANA has received significant investment, is reasonably trained, and is somewhat moving towards independent operations. It is perceived as a legitimate force by Helmandis that does not have tribal allegiances. However, its operational tempo is high, it is overstretched, and it suffers from high absenteeism. Large numbers of ANA troops surged to Helmand for Operation Moshtarak, together with the well-respected Afghan National Civil Order Police (ANCOP), but these numbers are likely to fall as the focus moves to other operational areas.

National Directorate of Security (NDS)

The National Directorate of Security (NDS) is Afghanistan's domestic security agency that is run by Amrullah Saleh, a Panjshiri Tajik from the north of Afghanistan, who is well regarded for his intellect by Western diplomats. Since 2001, the NDS has made significant progress towards becoming an effective intelligence agency. Many of its members are former Communist-era government officials. Pashtuns often claim that it is dominated by Tajiks. The NDS has faced criticism from international human rights groups and Western media organizations for alleged torture of suspects, particularly Taliban fighters held at its Kandahar headquarters. The NDS is thought to have some good human intelligence networks, but relies on Western technological assistance for electronic intelligence gathering. In Helmand, the commander of the NDS was General Naeem, who was transferred to another post in April

2010; at the time of writing the post is vacant. The NDS in Helmand is seen as underfunded and undertrained by some British officials. NDS officers are frequent targets of the Taliban which regularly kills anyone it believes to be NDS agents, usually with great cruelty.

Afghan National Police (ANP)

There are three main policing organizations in Helmand: the Afghan Uniformed Police (AUP), colloquially referred to as the "ANP"; the Afghan National Civil Order Police (ANCOP); and the Afghan Border Police (ABP). The AUP is currently a quasi-military force which is competent in basic life-saving battlefield skills, guarding, patrolling, and the provision of a low-level of security. ANCOP is more highly trained (16 weeks compared with the AUP's 8 weeks) and is designed for COIN and civil disturbances; it works closely with the ANA. The ABP is another quasi-military force designed to control borders. All the police are under the command of the Ministry of Interior in Kabul and do not report to Governor Mangal. Each separate force also has its own chain of command and there is limited interaction between the three at a provincial level.

Since 2001, the AUP has acquired an extremely poor reputation in many parts of the country. "Robbers with uniforms" is just one of their nick-names in Helmand. Their members have a reputation for routine bribery, extortion, criminality, and incompetence. Narcotics abuse is a problem in many police units, as is sexual abuse. Indeed, the AUP is more feared than the Taliban in some areas. Its leadership is weak and there is limited engagement by Kabul in the allocation of officers to Helmand. In addition Helmand's low levels of literacy hampers the growth of the NCO and officer cadres, as well as specialist branches.

According to accepted COIN ratios, 7,000 AUP officers would be required to wage an effective campaign in Helmand. However, the AUP's

tashkiel (authorized strength) is only 4,100 in the province. These officers are not available for duty, and a large proportion of them have not
received any training. Its provincial leadership is very mixed, with only
a few district chiefs of police having been assessed as competent. The
AUP's reputation varies across the province; in areas where they are
associated with specific tribally-based strongmen, they are detested –
as in Marja, where the AUP was historically loyal to Abdul Rahman Jan,
the Noorzai ex-police chief and malignant tribal strongman.

Newly trained officers are much better received in other areas. The
interim Helmand Police Training Academy is up and running, with
new recruits graduating at a rate of 150 every four weeks. Courses
are delivered by the British military and civilian police instructors, as
well as by the ANP. A permanent police academy is expected to be
completed in May 2011. The AUP's Crimestoppers telephone line has
proved a success. Established at the newly built police headquarters,
it encourages members of the public to contact their local police. Over
1,060 calls a week are processed; a planned upgrade of the telephone
system will allow more.

By contrast, the ANCOP has mature logistics and command structures to
enable its deployment to challenging areas. It also has much better leadership, though it still benefits from partnering with international forces.
Seen as a national force, the ANCOP is respected by the population and
plays a key role in major operations. During Operation Moshtarak, 700
ANCOP troops deployed to Marja and Nad Ali.

Militias

Often security and law enforcement falls to militias that have official
or semi-official status in the south of Afghanistan. In Helmand, these
include a number of anti-Taliban militias linked to old jihadi commanders.

Commander Koka, a Musa Qala commander loyal to Sher Mohammad Akhundzada, leads one such militia. He and his unit have been given official police status and were sent to police reform training. Another militia loyal to Abdul Rahman Jan operates in Marja district. It was commanded by Commander Toor Jan, who was killed in the summer of 2008. The militia lost control of Nad Ali in September 2008, but Western officials claim that the units deliberately abandoned their posts to the Taliban as part of a strategy to undermine the authority of the new governor of Helmand and promote the reinstatement of Sher Mohammad Akhundzada and Abdul Rahman Jan.

In addition to the formal security forces, many political and tribal leaders have armed security detachments which serve as bodyguards and security forces for their compounds. In some cases, their size is equal to small militias and their activities are often not well controlled. Efforts to disarm these groups have not made significant progress in Helmand.

Security Coordination

The security players in the province – Afghan Uniformed Police (AUP), Afghan National Army (ANA), National Directorate for Security (NDS), Afghan Border Police (ABP), and Counter Narcotics Police of Afghanistan(CNPA) – meet on a weekly basis with the governor, the PRT, and other US or ISAF soldiers to discuss security issues in the province. Emergency security meetings are held as required. The Operational Coordination Center (OCC)is staffed with liaison officers from every Afghan and ISAF security force, enabling security forces to coordinate quickly. The OCC is located in the governor's compound in Lashkar Gah and is a 24-hour operation.

LEADER PROFILES

Government and Political Leaders

There is regular turnover in provincial appointees by the central government. This is a long established tactic of the Afghan central government
to prevent individuals from establishing networks which would allow
corruption in their offices. In Helmand, violence and assassination often
end political careers. Below are the key political figures in Helmand as of
May 2010.

Governor Gulab Mangal: Gulab Mangal replaced Governor Assadullah
Wafa in March 2008. Mangal is from eastern Afghanistan and is the
former governor of Paktika and Laghman. He arrived in Helmand with
an impressive reputation and brought with him a team that included his
brother and brother-in-law.

Governor Mangal appears to have won respect in the province for his
honesty and his willingness to work with local political bodies. He is also
greatly liked by Western military commanders who see him as energetic
and principled. However, there is continual political pressure to remove
him from office by a number of powerbrokers in the province, particularly
Sher Mohammad Akhundzada and Abdul Rahman Jan. Mangal says
his priorities are to open schools, reinvigorate the tribal jirga system of
conflict resolution, engage with tribes, engage with those Taliban who
are prepared to negotiate, and oppose the drug mafias and warlords.

In Mangal's two years in office he has transformed the governance of
Helmand, despite having no natural Helmandi powerbase.

Commander Koka, Police District Commander of Musa Qala:
Commander Koka is the most prominent of the remaining anti-Taliban
militia commanders who were linked to Sher Mohammad Akhundzada

and Abdul Rahman Jan. Koka and his militia were incorporated into the formal police structure in 2006. He is currently the police district commander for Musa Qala. He has been praised for his job performance by British military officials and enjoys strong support from members of the local tribal shura. Koka has survived numerous Taliban assassination attempts. He has reported links to the drug trade and his militia has, in the past, been accused of extra-judicial killing, criminality, drug smuggling, and frequent looting. Koka and his militia went through police reform training in early 2008.

Commander Mullah Abdul Salaam, District Governor of Musa Qala: Mullah Salaam was a mid-level Taliban commander who defected to the government's side shortly before the fall of Musa Qala in December 2007. This was in line with a British-backed policy of negotiation with Taliban elements deemed to be "moderate." Mullah Salaam was a relatively modest figure within the Taliban structure from the Pirzai sub-tribe of the Alizai tribe in the Musa Qala area. He is a lesser figure than "Gut" Mullah Salaam ("Lame" Mullah Salaam), a major Taliban commander operating in north Helmand, with whom he sometimes is confused. After the fall of Musa Qala, Mullah Salaam was made the district governor. He proved himself a charismatic orator with a taste for eye-catching gold slippers, but his militia has frequently been accused of criminality and he is regarded as an uncertain ally.

Members of the Meshrano Jirga: Meshrano Jirga members for Helmand are Sher Mohammad Akhundzada, Haji Mahboob Khan, Attaullah, Haji Talib, and Haji Abdul Wahid.

Members of the Wolesi Jirga: Elected Wolesi Jirga members are: Haji Wali Jan (son of Abdul Rahman Jan), Dad Mohammad Khan, Shaikh Nimatullah Ghafari, Haji Mir Wali Khan, Engineer Abdul Matin, and Haji Mohammad Anwar Khan. The female MPs are Nasima Niazi and Naz Parwan. New parliamentary elections will take place in September 2010.

Other Leaders

Sher Mohammad Akhundzada (SMA): Sher Mohammad Akhundzada
leads the Hasanai sub-tribe of the Alizai tribe. His family has dominated
Helmand politics since the 1980s through a combination of astute
exploitation of the drug trade, tribal politicking, and ruthless suppression
of opponents. Sher Mohammad was governor from 2001 until December
2005, when the British government made his removal a precondition
for the deployment of UK forces. During his period in office, he carved
up power in the province with a number of former rivals, chief among
them Abdul Rahman Jan. In 2005, Western forces discovered nine tons of
opium in Sher Mohammad's offices that he claimed to have impounded
from drug smugglers on behalf of the government.

Akhundzada was given a seat in the Meshrano Jirga (parliament's upper
house) by President Karzai, with whom he maintains good relations. They
are reputed to be related by marriage through Karzai's brother, Ahmad
Wali Karzai (Kandahar's most prominent political figure). President Karzai
has made a number of public attacks on British effectiveness in Helmand,
unfavorably comparing the levels of drug production and insurgency
since the arrival of British troops to the period of Akhundzada's rule. Sher
Mohammad possesses considerable personal charm and wit. He now
lives mainly in Kabul, but has frequently lobbied for his reappointment as
Helmand's governor. His successors have often accused him of trying to
undermine their authority in the province.

Abdul Rahman Jan (ARJ): Abdul Rahman Jan is a former militia leader
who seized power when the Taliban was overthrown in 2001. He is from
the Noorzai tribe and his seat of power is Marja, west of the provincial
capital Lashkar Gah. ARJ, as he is often known to Western officials, is
reputed to be heavily involved in the narcotics industry. In 2008, Western
counter-narcotics officials made a concerted effort to eradicate areas
under ARJ's control. They believe that they managed to destroy approxi-

mately 20 percent of his opium crop, but lost as many as 20 policemen to ambushes and roadside bombs in the process.

ARJ's son, Wali Jan, is a member of the Afghan parliament. ARJ's militia is still a significant force in Nad Ali and Marja districts. They are an anti-Taliban force with semi-official standing. ARJ's senior commander, Toor Jan, was killed in the summer of 2008. The Taliban took Marja during September 2008 and pushed into Nad Ali. Western officials allege that ARJ's militia ceded the area without a fight as part of a strategy to use the Taliban as a buttress against Western counter-narcotics operations. ISAF retook Marja in February 2010.

Dad Mohammad Khan: Dad Mohammad Khan is an Alokazai from the Sangin district of Helmand. During the Soviet invasion, he rose to prominence as a militia commander and he is often referred to by the nickname "Amir Dado." He was forced into exile and returned in 2001 to be rewarded with the post of provincial director of NDS. He was an opponent of the Taliban and noted for his extreme brutality towards Taliban prisoners. His family continue to dominate the area around Sangin, where his brother was appointed district governor after 2001. However, Mohammed Sheriff, the new district governor, offers a challenge to their position.

In June 2006, almost 50 members of Dad Mohammad's family were killed in an attack blamed on the Taliban. However, there have been persuasive, subsequent claims that the attack was primarily driven by the feud between Dad Mohammad and his clan and the local members of the Isakzai tribe. Dad Mohammad was dismissed in 2005 and now lives in Kabul. He is a member of the Wolesi Jirga.

An Afghan woman weaves a rug at a studio run by an NGO which sells rugs abroad to help families purchase healthcare and education, breaking the cycle of poverty.

PHOTO BY SGT. HEIDI AGOSTINI

Chapter 4
The Economy

H elmand is and always has been a largely agrarian economy, with farmers leveraging the fertile soil of the Helmand River delta. According to UNAMA's provincial profile from 2005, agriculture was a major source of revenue for 69 percent of households in the province. Trade, services, and crafts traditionally account for additional economic activity, providing income to about a quarter of Helmandi families.

Where Helmandi farmers once thrived on cash crops like wheat, tobacco, and cotton and benefited from government and international development plans, the harsh conditions of war and Taliban rule caused many to grow more food for subsistence and narcotics crops instead. Locals plant wheat, corn, fruit trees, and nut trees for survival and rely on poppy for currency, leveraging its durability and ease of distribution.

The infrastructure is poor by Western standards, but better than many other Afghan provinces, particularly in the electrical and communications sectors.

Three national retail bank branches have opened in Lashkar Gah since 2007. Over 3,000 loans, totaling $2 million have been dispersed to small businesses in the safer central districts.

AGRICULTURE

Farming is now done primarily for subsistence or for producing opium poppy, and transportation of commercial crops has become extremely difficult. Should violence decrease, an understanding of Helmand's economic past will be useful to plan for the province's recovery. There were two industrial crops traditionally grown in the province: cotton was produced in 57 percent of villages, mainly in Nad Ali, Nawa-i Barikzayi, and Garmser, and tobacco was produced in 24 percent of the villages, mostly in Garmser, Kajaki, Baghran, Nad Ali, and Nahre-Sarraj. There was also a scattering of sesame and sugar production. The most important food crops included wheat, maize, and melons. The most common crops grown in garden plots included fruit and nut trees and grapes.

War has not destroyed the rich agricultural land, and some very wealthy landowners have recovered. The best areas are those around Lashkar Gah, particularly Nad Ali and Marja to the west of the city, which are fed by US-designed irrigation systems. The same is true of Garmser to the south. However, areas outside the irrigation systems are marginal, and farmers who pump water from the water table with petrol generators have been hit hard by rising fuel prices. Many farmers grow poppy, but it should be noted that poppy is often part of a multi-crop program, so a field may be put to different uses in different seasons.

Cotton production is still encouraged by local powerbrokers in Helmand as an alternative to poppy, and a mill exists in Lashkar Gah. However, the British experiment with cotton in Helmand was largely a failure. Afghanistan simply cannot compete with its neighbors (India and Pakistan) to produce the quantity and quality of cotton necessary for exportation.

Agriculture will be the predominant economic sector in Helmand for the foreseeable future and will be the focus of economic assistance efforts. Because travel is so dangerous, assistance to farmers in obtaining seed and fertilizer and getting crops to market will be invaluable. Similarly, protection of irrigation systems and the crews attempting to repair them will be crucial.

Other Economic Sectors

Helmand's non-agricultural businesses have stagnated due to the condition of roads and continued insecurity. Marble quarries in the south of the province are of high quality, but are inaccessible due to the lack of roads. For this reason, much of Helmand's marble is smuggled to Pakistan. Local bazaars serve the needs of the people, providing them with goods like food, medicine, and local crafts.

INFRASTRUCTURE

Electricity

Helmand has two separate legacy power grids, based on the hydro-electric plants at Kajaki and Gereshk. The Kajaki hydroelectric power plant was added to the dam in 1975 (through USAID funding) and fed a subsidiary line to Musa Qala and a main line to Sangin, Durai Junction, and then to Kandahar. Another subsidiary line ran from Durai Junction to Lashkar Gah. The first turbine has been rehabilitated, with a significant improvement in electricity supply in Lashkar Gah. The rehabilitation of the second turbine was commissioned in October 2009 and is currently being worked on. Each turbine can generate 16.5 MW. The dam as a whole currently produces 33 MW and will reach a capacity of 51.5 MW when the newly-installed third turbine

Map. 3
Economic Map of Helmand

———	Roads
~~	District Border
———	River
⊙	Provincial Capital
●	City
▨	Arable Land
▨	Range Land
⟷	Trade Routes
▬	Marble Quarry
✈	Airfield
✈	Airstrip
⊢⊣	Kajaki Dam

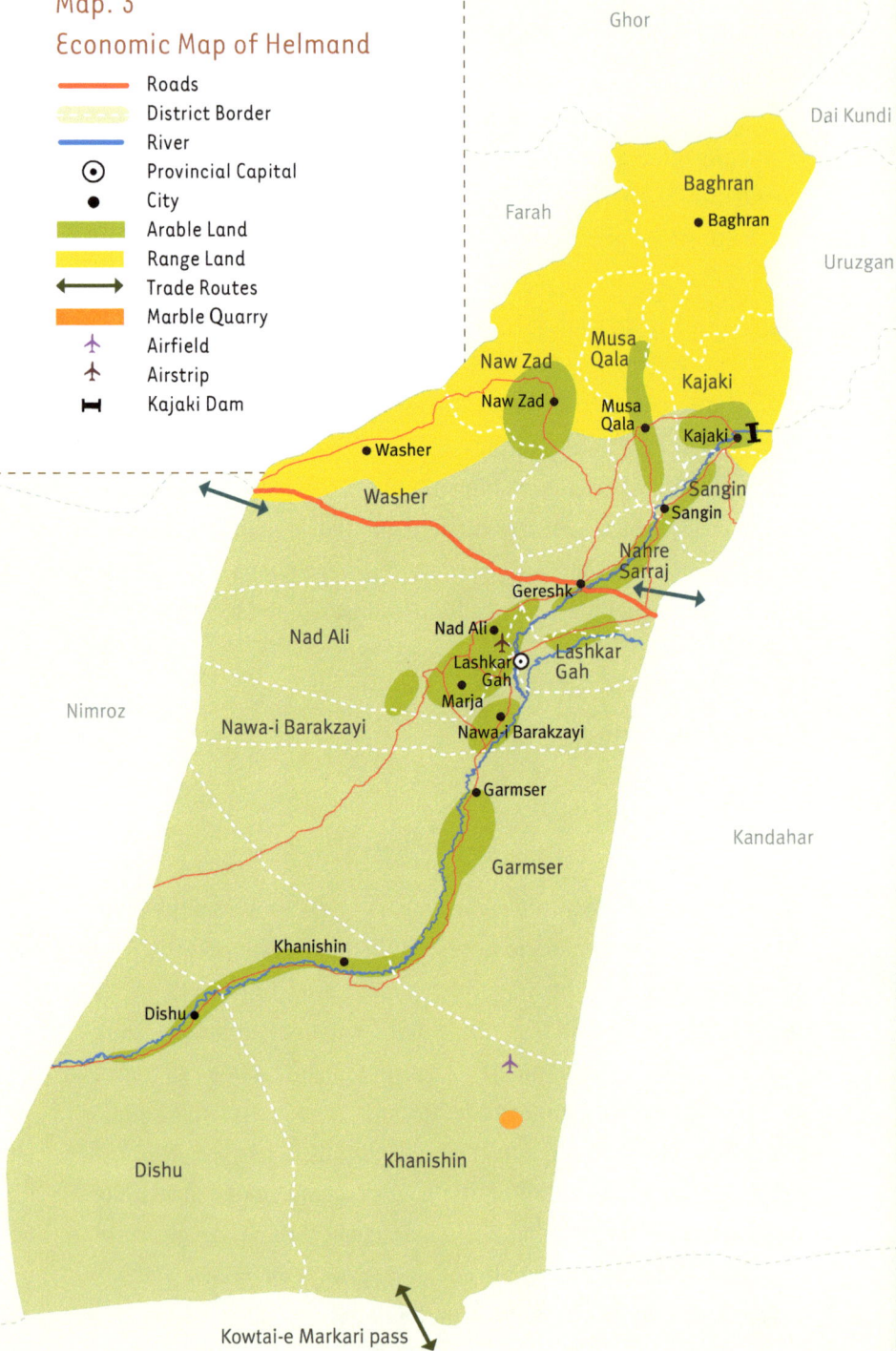

Ghor

Dai Kundi

Farah

Uruzgan

Baghran

● Baghran

Naw Zad

Musa Qala

Kajaki

Naw Zad ●

Musa Qala ●

Kajaki ●

● Washer

Washer

Sangin

● Sangin

Nahre Sarraj

Gereshk ●

Nad Ali

Nad Ali ●

Lashkar Gah

Lashkar Gah ⊙

Marja ●

Nimroz

Nawa-i Barakzayi

Nawa-i Barakzayi ●

Garmser ●

Kandahar

Garmser

Khanishin ●

Dishu ●

Khanishin

Dishu

Pakistan

Kowtai-e Markari pass

comes online. However, this additional capacity will be pushed to Kandahar City and there are no plans to extend this capacity to the rest of the province.

The Gereshk hydroelectric power plant was constructed in 1958 and is unserviceable. The PRT intends to rehabilitate the hydro-power plant and the smaller grid, but it was designed when Gereshk was much smaller and will now probably supply electricity just to that town.

In Nad Ali, Marja, Nawa, and Garmser districts there are some locations on the canal system where there is potential for mini- and micro-hydroelectric power generation, but these sites need to be surveyed and proper feasibility studies must be undertaken before any possible designs can be developed.

Muncipal Services

Solar-powered street lights have been and are being installed in all the district centers, and a DFID-funded UN habitat program is providing access to safe drinking water for some 35,000 people in Lashkar Gah by installing hand pumps and building new water towers.

Transportation

Helmand is not well endowed with roads. Highway 1, the national ring road, was upgraded during recent years. Route 601, the road that connects Lashkar Gah to Highway 1 and then to Kandahar, was rehabilitated three to four years ago.

The insecurity that affects all the main arteries in the south makes traveling difficult for Afghans and foreign nationals. The part of Highway 1 that runs through Helmand has been secured by the US Army's Stryker Brigade. However, many Afghan businessmen complain about the predatory behavior of police. Extortion at police checkpoints is considered routine. This, in tandem with high levels of banditry on remote stretches of land, has created a situation engaging in commerce is risky and is often only possible at great cost to a well-connected mafia monitoring transportation.

Airfield

A $50 million contract was put up for tender in September 2008 to build a 2-km runway and airport infrastructure on the site of an undeveloped airstrip at Bost, outside Lashkar Gah. It was completed and Bost Airport now receives 40 flights a week; a Helmandi can fly to Kabul for $60. It is operated and secured by Afghans.

Education

The Ministry of Education in Kabul – resourced with international and national technical advisors – develops policies and programs to be implemented at the provincial level. Denmark is responsible for assisting the Provincial Education Department, which is active in 10 districts. The school year starts in September and finishes in May. The school year starts with better attendance which drops away in January. The latest figures, from January 2010, show total enrolment of 83,995 pupils, 64,846 male and 19,149 female. This represents an increase of 635 since December 2007. Female reenrollment in particular has dramatically increased, up by 34% during this period. 40 new schools have re-opened across Helmand since 2008, bringing the total to 103. There are 1,772 teachers, 341 of whom are female. A teacher training college has been established in Lashkar Gah.

Health

Healthcare in Afghanistan is delivered in each province by an NGO implementing the Basic Package of Health Services (BPHS) under the direction of the Ministry of Public Health. In Helmand this is undertaken by the Bangladeshi Rural Advancement Committee (BRAC). BRAC now operates clinics in all priority district centers. In 2006, there was one district hospital, nine Comprehensive Health Clinics and 20 Basic Health Clinics. In 2009, this increased to two district hospitals, 15 Comprehensive Health Clinics, 30 Basic Health Clinics, and nine Sub Centers. Over 300 Health Posts operate across the province, providing basic health care at a local level, and now 80 percent of the population lives within five miles of some form of medical treatment. Though all the basic metrics have improved, they are still shockingly bad, primarily driven by a lack of appropriately trained medical personnel.

A Marine supporting a bridge construction project in northern Marja greets locals who have come to observe the process.

PHOTO BY LANCE CPL. KHOA PELCZAR

Chapter 5
Reconstruction Activities
and International Organizations

G iven the volatile security situation, traditional development
programming – focused on medium- and long-term impacts – is not
possible in many areas of the province. Instead, flexible, quick impact
types of activities are required to respond to the constantly changing
situation on the ground. Small projects – often simple infrastructure
repairs for roads, schools, and irrigation systems – are used to create
short-term employment in local communities, providing a much needed
infusion of cash while building trust with the local people. The British
military has used its quick-impact funding to complete a variety of
projects – particularly in the strategic corridors between Lashkar Gah
and Gereshk and between Gereshk and Sangin. The US Agency for
International Development (USAID) and the Afghan Ministry of Rural
Reconstruction and Development (MRRD) have used similar programming models to complete activities in the wake of military operations in
Sangin and Musa Qala. Close coordination between civilian and military
counterparts is essential for success, especially in insecure areas where
military operations may be ongoing.

Another area of focus for civilian development agencies is governance
capacity-building programs. Civilian development agencies have focused
on improving the capacity of Afghan government institutions at the

sub-national level to increase stability at the provincial and district levels. Improving the professional abilities of Afghan officials and their staffs to deliver services and build confidence in their government would also build confidence in local authorities and separate the population from insurgents. In Helmand, efforts by both the British and American governments to build the capacity of local government institutions has been hampered by the relative insecurity in many of Helmand's districts and the constant turnover of governors. The arrival of Governor Mangal in the spring of 2008 caused donors to provide much needed upgrades to government facilities, equipment, and training at the provincial level for both line ministries and the governor's office. In addition, both the US and the UK have pledged to build or upgrade facilities at the district level and provide training to district-level officials.

The Ministry of Rural Rehabilitation has resurfaced 72 km of roads, predominantly in Lashkar Gah, as well as 10 km in the district centers of Garmser, Nad Ali, Sangin, Musa Qala, and Gereshk. Major road-building projects include:

- Lashkar Gah to Gereshk, 48 km, construction expected to start in late 2010

- Lashkar Gah to Garmser, 81km, construction ongoing

- Lashkar Gah to Nad Ali, 10km, construction ongoing

- Highway 1 link to Sangin, construction ongoing, funded by the United Arab Emirates

- Garmser ring road, planned for CERP funding

- Lashkar Gah to Nawa, planned for CERP funding

PROVINCIAL RECONSTRUCTION TEAM (PRT)

The PRT, formally the Civil-Military Mission in Helmand, is different from other PRTs in Afghanistan. It is civilian-led, is the largest PRT in Afghanistan, and has UK, US, Danish, and Estonian participation. The PRT in Lashkar Gah and its satellite District Stabilization Teams (DSTs) have almost 250 staff – half civilian and half military. The PRT includes some 30 civilian police staff and 30 Afghan staff. It is currently commanded by a British civilian "two-star" with a US deputy. The PRT helps the Afghan government deliver effective governance and security across the province. The PRT is funded by the UK, US, Danish, and Estonian governments and has access to more than $500 million in funding from international sources.

Large groups from the PRT focus on politics, governance, rule of law, counter-narcotics, health, education, and infrastructure. They work with Governor Mangal, the line ministries, and, through 10 DSTs, the district governors. The PRT budget for these projects was £33.4 million ($50 million) in September 2010.

In addition, District Stabilization Teams exist in Gereshk (Nahri Saraj district), Garmser, Sangin, Musa Qala, Nad Ali, Marja, Nawa, and Khanishin (Reg district), and have a presence in Now Zad. A DST consists of civilian stabilization advisers, civilian specialists (i.e. in agriculture), a political adviser, and a military stabilization support team, which brings together military personnel with a range of backgrounds, including development, politics, engineering, and project management. Each DST works closely with the district's battle space owner to coordinate civil and military activity.

USAID, the UK Department for International Development (DFID), and Danish representatives sit within the Civil-Military Mission in Helmand, but have development programs separate from those of the PRT:

USAID delivered $282.4 million in development support to Helmand between 2002 and 2008; DFID has set aside $115 million for programs in Helmand between 2009 and 2013; and Denmark earmarked $7.5m for education in Helmand. The UK's Afghan Drugs Interdepartmental Unit also spent £6.2 million ($10 million) in the last financial year.

The PRT has been active in supporting the agriculture sector. $1.3 million worth of improvements has been made to the Shamalan canal, improving irrigation for 10,000 farmers. Mercy Corps has built a brand new agriculture high school that provides vocational training for 600 students aged 16 to 18. Five-hundred thousand fruit tree saplings and grape vines were distributed to 1,240 farmers in Garmser, Nawa, Lashkar Gah, and Gereshk. Thirty-five thousand farmers have received training and a further 15,700 have received seed and fertilizer. Thirty-nine co-operatives have received training and equipment grants. Establishing such co-operatives has been a relative success, especially at providing grain storage facilities. The PRT actively avoids providing farmers with micro-grants for operational costs and consumable goods or funding unsustainable new technologies. Cold storage is a reccurring demand, but is again viewed as unsustainable. DFID is financing the further development of the Agricultural Business Park adjacent to the new airport at Bost.

NATIONAL SOLIDARITY PROGRAM

The National Solidarity Program (NSP) is the $600 million flagship development program of the Ministry of Rural Rehabilitation and Development (MRRD). It is a rural reconstruction program conducted at the village level, with the decision-making process given to the villagers themselves.

Under the NSP, villages elect their own Community Development Councils (CDCs), which then vote on their development priorities. Having finalized a Community Development Plan, the village must make a contribution of approximately 10 percent of the cost in labor, funds, or material before it receives a grant up to $60,000. The labor is generally provided by the villagers, while the expertise is provided by an implementing partner, usually an NGO.

However, NSP has not worked in Helmand, primarily because of the security situation. The Bangladeshi NGO BRAC is the implementing partner, but most CDCs it established have completed one project and then faded away.

A Special Forces commander meets with village elders to discuss military operations in the Sangin district. Sangin has recently gained attention as the site of battles between British ISAF forces and the Taliban. ISAF has secured the town but not the surrounding countryside.

PHOTO BY PAT IRISH

Chapter 6
Information and Influence

L iteracy rates in Helmand are low. The primary way in which news travels is by word of mouth: gossiping at the bazaar, talking over green tea among groups of elders, or listening to the pulpit in the local mosque. This makes Helmand a peculiarly fertile ground for rumor, exaggeration, and disinformation.

While Helmand has a relatively sophisticated urban minority, many Helmandis are from isolated rural communities and may never have been to the provincial capital, let alone the country capital. Their world-view is often very limited. As noted in Chapter 5, Helmand is rife with conspiracy theories and rumors about Western intentions in Afghanistan.

TELECOMMUNICATIONS

There are no significant landline networks in Helmand. Since 2001, mobile phone companies have installed a network of mobile phone masts covering much of the inhabited area in the center of the province, and district centers in parts of the north. Many Helmandis have been able to buy mobile phones, and this has changed the dynamics of local culture, allowing much faster dissemination of information and better organization of people's lives.

The main providers are AWCC and Roshan, with AfTel, the government-owned provider, having only a very small footprint around Lashkar Gah. Although the Helmandis have embraced mobile telephones, the Taliban believe ISAF track their locations through cell phones. A spate of attacks on the operators' staff and installations in 2009 led to a retrenchment of services, which are slowly creeping back as security allows. However, the mobile telephone operators remain vulnerable – their staff and facilities in Helmand can be protected, but this is not true across the rest of the country. For instance, the Taliban can easily attack an unguarded relay station in Farah and achieve the same result.

MEDIA

There are a number of radio stations broadcasting in Helmand, and wind-up radios are popular with local people. RTA, Radio Sabaun, Radio Samoon ,Radio Bost, and Radio Mushkab all broadcast from Lashkar Gah, but have a limited footprint around the capital and into Nad Ali. Radio Mushkab, a new radio station run by and catering towards women, is also notable. These are all FM stations. AM broadcasts, such as the BBC World Service's Pashto channel, are severely hampered by the mountainous geography.

The Institute for War and Peace Reporting (IWPR), a media training NGO, opened an office in Lashkar Gah and has trained a number of local journalists, several of whom now work for the BBC in Helmand and other international media. The IWPR program ended in the summer of 2008.

Television is also popular, but reception is limited and television sets are expensive.

Governor Mangal's team makes good use of the media. Helmand has the only government media center outside Kabul, and while capabilities are in developmental stages, it still is far more advanced than most Afghan provinces.

The local press corps is small and tight-knit. In June 2008 Abdul Samad Rohani, a local journalist working for the BBC and for the IWPR, was kidnapped and murdered in Lashkar Gah. His death has seriously impacted the movement of other journalists who had previously reported from Taliban-held areas. Local reporters now conceal their identities on many of the more controversial articles they write. It is not clear whether the Taliban were responsible for the death of Rohani; local rumor suggests that it was likely the work of local political figures.

The Taliban has developed an effective propaganda arm, delivering their messages primarily through sympathetic mullahs at Friday prayers, night letters in villages, cassettes of pro-Taliban songs widely sold in bazaars, DVDs containing messages, footage of Taliban fighters and executions of pro-government spies, and even recently through the sale of Taliban mobile phone ringtones.

A US Marine patrols a poppy field in Garmsir district. Because farmers do not have to travel to markets to sell opium, dealers pay advances on the crop, and opium can be stored up to two years, poppy production remains extremely attractive to many farmers.

PHOTO BY MARK O'DONALD

Chapter 7
The Big Issues

SECURITY AND VIOLENCE

Security is the dominant issue in Helmand, and the other big issues are intricately tied to the security situation. The past two years have seen a steadily improving security situation in the central population areas, but there was a very low starting point. The Taliban now have less freedom of movement in Nawa, Nad Ali, Lashkar Gah, and Gereshk, where 70 percent of the population lives, and increasingly use IEDs and political assassination of GIRoA supporters. The security situation is still very dangerous outside of those districts.

The ongoing fighting in the province since 2006 has led to significant loss of life and internal displacement of the local populace in some areas, while pro-government figures have been forced to flee to the provincial capital for safety from Taliban retribution. The deterioration of security is most pronounced in areas which are being contested by the government and the Taliban. In these areas, heavy fighting has allowed criminal elements to exploit the situation. The police are also responsible for widespread criminality and extortion, particularly along the roadways. Local tribal militias also operate in some areas and are accused of criminal behavior.

The insecurity on the highways has had a negative impact on legal agriculture in the province. With the added expense of bribery and the risk to those transporting goods, the cost of getting produce to markets is high. Some farmers are reported to have allowed produce to rot in their fields because of the risks involved in moving it.

Security, of a sort, is generally better in Taliban-held areas, with low levels of criminality due to the Taliban's brutal, but effective form of justice. Taliban courts operate in these areas and local people frequently use them to arbitrate disputes. However, the Taliban are often cruel in their treatment of local people, particularly when they suspect that spies have been passing information to the government or Western forces. They engage in frequent summary executions of anyone they suspect of working for the government or receiving Western aid, and they often harass or kill tribal elders.

The population widely resent it when Taliban bands burn schools, tax the local population under the pretense of "zakat" (charity), or demand food and shelter. When Taliban fighters stay in villages, there is also the risk of NATO military action and harm to local civilians.

In the summer of 2008, the Taliban dropped many of its unpopular social laws, such as the forced growing of beards and bans on music, television, kite flying, dog fighting, and other popular local entertainments in a general attempt to broaden its popularity. The Taliban also courts popularity by allowing poppy cultivation.

In many towns, the local population is at risk from widely detested Taliban suicide bombings. Afghan authorities report that local people frequently provide information to the authorities on suspected bombers.

THE TALIBAN

The Taliban movement leads the insurgency under the banner of jihad against foreign occupation. Their goal is an emirate under Mullah Omar who styles himself Emir al-Mu'mineen, leader of faithful Muslims, irrespective of nationality. They appeal to Helmandis' religious and independent spirit, and if that does not work, they fall back on intimidation and pragmatism – paying people to pick up a weapon – for their support.

The Taliban in Helmand is not having an easy time. Mid- and senior-level commanders are regularly killed or captured and the greatly increased ISAF presence, with the arrival of 1 MEF, increasingly challenges their position. There are early signs of an appetite, among some low level fighters, for reintegration, but this should not be over-exaggerated.

There is no strong correlation between tribal membership and Taliban membership. When certain prominent fighters join the Taliban, others from their tribe may follow them and create pockets of members from one tribe within the Taliban, but all tribes are represented on both sides of the struggle.

CRIMINALITY

A significant source of violence and instability in Helmand is widespread criminality. It is particularly prevalent on roads in areas of weak government control. Sometimes it is linked to figures who claim to be Taliban, to militias, or to the Afghan police (a force with a reputation for low morale, low pay, and low caliber recruits). The effect of such corruption is to exacerbate the sense of insecurity among the populace and to seriously hinder the movement of goods and people around the province.

JUSTICE

There are a variety of venues for justice in Helmand and they do not comple-
ment each other. There are the formal state institutions, informal mechanisms
(like the DCC's justice sub-committees), community-based dispute resolution
mechanisms, and, of course, the Taliban. The community processes are based
on village shuras and the pashtunwali code of behavior and resolve the vast
majority of disputes. The Taliban compete with these, seeking to dominate
justice delivery in their provinces, and while their "shadow courts" undoubt-
edly are tough on crime, they are heavy-handed, ruthless, and arbitrary.

Each of the four existing District Community Councils has a justice sub-
committee to provide for community-based dispute resolution and acts as a
crucial link between the formal and informal justice mechanisms, providing
support to community peace and the rule of law. This will be extended across
the province over the coming year.

A new provincial chief justice was appointed in the summer of 2008, with a
rolling program providing prosecutors in Sangin, Gereshk, and Garmser. The
most recent appointment was to Nad Ali in February 2010. However, there are
only two defense lawyers in Helmand.

In October 2009, Helmand's run-down prison was replaced with the first wing
of a new, purpose-built facility. It will house up to four hundred prisoners
in an environment that is more secure and meets international standards.
The prison build is scheduled for completion in November 2010. A block for
female prisoners has also been completed, and a juvenile detention facility
will be built alongside the adult prison.

OPIUM CULTIVATION

As drug production has dropped in parts of the east and north of the country,
it has continued in the insurgency-ridden south, highlighting the mutually
supportive relationship between instability and narco-criminality. According

to the UNODC's Winter Assessment, opium cultivation in Helmand in 2010 is expected to remain stable at around 100,000 hectares, still over 50% of the total production in Afghanistan. The 2010 yield, however, is expected to be lower due to drought and disease affecting the crop. Opium offers a number of advantages for farmers over other crops. Unlike legal crops, farmers do not have to face the uncertainty and danger of transporting their crop to market through a war zone because opium dealers come to them. In addition, many farmers are able to sell their crops in advance under a system by which the dealers pay an advance to farmers in return for the guarantee to sell to them. While the advance is between 35 percent and 50 percent of the true value of the crop, it gives many poorer farmers a source of income through the winter. A further advantage to opium is that it can be stored up to two years while holding its value, which, in a fluctuating priced market, allows the farmer to seek the best price for his crop. The farmers also do not need to worry about protection from local militias and corrupt police, as the Taliban protects them and takes its cut from the cartel.

Efforts to counter the drug problem have combined carrot and stick tactics: the promotion of "alternative livelihoods" for farmers on the one hand and the threat of Afghan police-led eradication on the other. Governor Mangal's Counter-Narcotics Strategy (also known as the Food Zone Program) contributed to a 33 percent reduction in opium cultivation in Helmand in 2009. The Food Zone Program, the first provincial strategy of its kind, provides agricultural inputs, like seed and fertilizer, to farmers in the central irrigated districts. Combined with the threat of some eradication, it has forced opium cultivation to more marginal areas.

In 2008, as part of this strategy, 3,200 tons of wheat seed was distributed to 32,000 farmers across the province, supporting a transition to legal livelihoods. In 2009, 37,500 farmers across Helmand received wheat seed and fertilizer. This was followed in February 2010 with the distribution of fruit saplings (apricots, plums, and pomegranates) and vines to nearly 1,200 famers, together with agricultural advice.

The latest phase of the program took place in the spring of 2010. Up to 27,000 farmers received subsidized agricultural inputs, giving them a chance to boost their agribusiness and household income and reducing the farmers' dependency on poppy cultivation. This distribution has been focused on Marja, enabling the Afghan government to deliver tangible, consent-winning services to those affected by Operation Moshtarak. Government-led eradication has been operating in areas where security conditions allow and where access to alternative livelihoods has been provided previously. This injects credible risk into farmers' future planting decisions.

Cultivation is down from the highs of 2007, but this was as much due to economics as government initiatives. The price of opium fell decisively in 2008 and 2009, suggesting that after three years during which Afghanistan produced an estimated 30 percent more than the world market for heroin, the world's drug economy is catching up with the demand. This, in combination with worldwide rises in food prices, particularly the wheat market, saw a shift towards growing legal crops in 2008. The high price of oil has also affected the underlying cost of poppy production in Helmand because many farmers without access to the irrigation system along the Helmand River must fuel generators to pump water from below ground. However, the wheat price has fallen and the opium price has increased over 2009 and 2010.

RELATIONS WITH INTERNATIONAL FORCES.

There is an undercurrent of xenophobia among southern Pashtuns and a mistrust of Great Britain because of historical confrontations. Though this seems strange to many Westerners, it is entirely plausible to southern Pashtuns that the British have returned to exact revenge for past defeats. There is a Pashto proverb that states: "I took my revenge after 100 years and thought I was quick about it."

Therefore, it is unsurprising that the arrival of British forces in Helmand in 2006 was met with suspicion. The heavy fighting that followed, and particularly the decision by British commanders to put troops into a number of district centers, quickly aroused local anger, particularly after the small forces available to deploy had to request the use of unpopular air support to hold their positions. In Musa Qala, Sangin, Kajaki, and Gereshk, there was considerable displacement of the population and also bombing damage.

Many Helmandis have viewed the failure of UK forces to drive out the Taliban with bemusement. "With all the technology and all the force that they have at their disposal," goes the popular line in the Helmand bazaars, "how could they fail to defeat the Taliban, who only have RPGs and AK-47s? The answer must be that they don't want to win."

In a country where conspiracy theories find fertile ground, the current theories in Helmand include plots to maintain a Western military presence by keeping the war going, to suppress and humiliate Pashtuns in revenge for Britain's 19th century defeats, to steal Helmand's opium industry, or to keep a strategic base for exploiting Afghan and other Central Asian resources (including uranium, which is rumored to be present in Helmand). Amongst many Helmandis, these are regarded as highly plausible theories and have been bolstered by rumors of Western helicopters seen dropping supplies to Taliban insurgents.

Many of the conspiracy theories are extended to the increased US presence. Many Helmandis believe that the US has ulterior motives, whether to gain access to natural resources, to build pipelines, or to secure permanent bases.

Marine mentors instruct ANBP soldiers on proper weapons handling as part of a program to build better training techniques.

PHOTO BY: LANCE CPL. BRANDYN E. COUNCIL

Appendices

TIMELINE OF KEY EVENTS IN HELMAND SINCE RESURGENCE OF TALIBAN

December 2005: Sher Mohammad Akhundzada replaced as governor of Helmand by Governor Mohammad Daoud.

May 2006: British troops from 16 Air Assault Brigade arrive in Helmand and initially deploy to Lashkar Gah and Gereshk.

May-June 2006: Taliban fighters attack Sangin, Naw Zad, and Musa Qala; British forces deployed to "Platoon Houses" in Musa Qala, Sangin, Naw Zad, and, later, Garmser.

June-September 2008: Heavy fighting around Musa Qala, Sangin, Naw Zad and Garmser.

September 2006: Musa Qala Deal. In a deal negotiated between tribal elders and Musa Qala leaders, the elders agree to exclude the Taliban from the town and a 5 km radius around it. Fighting stops in Musa Qala, and a month later British troops withdraw from the area.

December 2006: Assadullah Wafa replaces Mohammad Daoud as governor of Helmand.

February 2007: Musa Qala Deal breaks down and the Taliban openly reoccupy the town.

April 2007: British and US forces break the siege of the district center in Sangin.

June-September 2007: British forces engage Taliban in a number of sweep operations between Gereshk and Sangin.

December 2007: British and US forces retake the town of Musa Qala.

March 2008: Gulab Mangal replaces Assadullah Wafa as governor of Helmand.

April-May 2008: US Marines push Taliban out of fixed positions south of Garmser.

September 2008: Taliban occupy Marja and large parts of Nad Ali district west of Lashkar Gah.

February 2010: US Marine units clear Marja in Operation Moshtarak and establish GIRoA control of the area.

June 2010: 1 MEF takes command of the British taskforce and forms RC South-West

COMMON COMPLIMENTS REGARDING ISAF SOLDIERS

- International forces try to bring security.

- International forces do not steal from the people like local security forces and the government, and they try to be honest with the people.

- Afghans respect ISAF soldiers for leaving their families to come and help them.

- Helmandis particularly respect Americans above other foreign nationals because of the Helmand River project which transformed the province into highly productive farmland in the 1950s to 1970s.

- Afghans compliment the US forces' work ethic and say it drives them to work harder for themselves.

- Afghans are happy for projects such as roads that change their lives for the better after decades of war.

COMMON COMPLAINTS REGARDING ISAF SOLDIERS

- Afghans claim that international forces lack respect for culture and traditions. This includes a lack of respect and understanding regarding women and the way they should be treated.

- Afghans complain that ISAF soldiers enter people's homes without the permission of the homeowner, which is a grave attack on the honor of an Afghan man and an insult to the women of the home.

- Afghans claim that when international forces are attacked by insurgents, they sometimes retaliate against innocent people, particularly with airstrikes. Also, they take out too few insurgent leaders while causing civilian casualties.

- Afghans believe international forces use informers for their intelligence gathering who are not being honest. Most of these people have their own agendas and manipulate the truth.

- Afghans believe that too much international aid goes to "rich" or corrupt individuals.

- Afghans complain about the lack of security and rule of law. Helmandis, in particular, lament the lack of patrols or security outside of major towns.

DAY IN THE LIFE OF A RURAL HELMANDI

The life of a rural Helmandi starts very early in the morning with the Imam's call to prayer one hour before sunrise. Men of the family get up and wash in accordance with Islamic tradition before going to their village mosque for the first of five prayers of the day. Women pray at home, start a fire, and prepare breakfast. Young boys and girls receive religious instruction at the local mosque after the prayer and before breakfast. In most houses in Helmand, breakfast is just green tea and bread. This might be supplemented with milk and butter for those who have cattle. Sugar is usually served only to guests.

After breakfast, men go to the field. Families prepare children for school if one is available (this is more likely in the cities and towns than in the country). Boys are far more likely to attend schools than girls. If they are not in school, young boys and girls who have not reached physical maturity help to graze the cattle. The older boys help their fathers in the field. All the children also help with the maize and opium poppy harvests. Migrant laborers are also often hired for the poppy harvest, which is very labor intensive. As a consequence, insurgent activity tends to fall at this time.

Women do not work outside the home and do not leave the family compound unless it is to visit relatives or attend weddings or festivals. Sometimes, on Fridays, women meet to sing or recite the Koran. In villages where there is no tension between families, women will not wear the burqa and will speak to men from other families. If there are local tensions, there will often be no interaction between families. Usually, everyone returns home for lunch at midday, but sometimes men will stay in the field. A typical lunch for Helmandis is rice with cooked vegetables, which is often accompanied by yogurt and slices of onion or other kinds of fresh vegetables from the fields; meat will be served if it is available. If a family kills a sheep, it will usually share meat with its neighbors. In north Helmand, there is a tradition of salting and drying mutton. It is too hot to store meat in the south of the province. Families will usually store pomegranates, almonds, and grapes to supplement their diet during the winter months.

FURTHER READING AND SOURCES

Books

- *ISAF PRT Handbook*, 3rd Ed. February 2007. NATO.

- Louis Dupree, *Afghanistan*, Princeton: Princeton University Press, 1979. (Available in paperback and excellent understanding of the code of Pahstuns. Understand Pashtunwali and you will be successful.)

- Edward Girardet and Jonathan Walter, *Afghanistan: Essential Field Guides to Humanitarian and conflict zones*, CROSSLINES Publication Ltd., 1998 and 2004.

- Ahmed Rashid, *Taliban: Militant Islam, Oil and Fundamentalism in Central Asia*, 2001.

- Larry Goodson, *Afghistan's Endless War: State Failure, Regional Politics, and the Rise of the Taliban*, 2001.

- Barnett Rubin, 1) *The Fragmentation of Afghanistan* and 2) *Afghanistan's Uncertain Transition from Turmoil to Normalcy*, 2001 and 2007

- Michael Griffin, *Reaping the Whirlwind: The Taliban Movement in Afghanistan*, London: Pluto Press, 2001.

- Steve Coll, *Ghost Wars*: *The Secret History of the CIA, Afghanistan, and Bin Laden, From the Soviet Invasion to September 10, 2001*, New York Penquin Press, 2004.

- Ben Macintyre, *The Man Who Would Be King, The First American in Afghanistan,* New York: Farrar, Straus and Giroux, 2005.

Articles

- Asger Christensen. "The Pashtuns of Kunar: Tribe, Class, and Community Organization," *Afghanistan Journal,* Vol. 7, No. 3, 1980.

- The Afghanistan National Development Strategy, President Karzai, 2006, *www.reliefweb.int/rw/RWFiles2006.nsf/ FilesByRWDocUNIDFileName/KHII-6LK3R2-unama-afg-30jan2. pdf/$File/unama-afg-30jan2.pdf*

- *Mines and Mineral Occurrences of Afghanistan*, compiled by G.H. Orris and J.D. Bliss, open-file report 02-110, U.S. Geological Survey, U.S. Department of the Interior, 2002.

Web Sites

- Afghanistan Research and Evaluation Unit (publishes the *Afghanistan A to Z* guide), *www.areu.org.af/index. php?option=com_frontpage&Itemid=25*

- Afghanistan Information Management Services, *www.aims.org.af*

- Afghanstan Online (Links to Official IRA and embassy websites), *www.afghan-web.com/politics*

- Naval Postgraduate School Program for Culture and Conflict Studies, *www.nps.edu/Programs/CCS/index.html*

- USAID, *www.usaid.gov/locations/asia/countries/afghanistan*